Authors

Henri Krishna is a welfare rights worker with the Advising BME Communities project at CPAG in Scotland.
Simon Osborne is a welfare rights worker at CPAG.
Mark Willis is a welfare rights worker with the Tax Credits and Early Years project at CPAG in Scotland.

Acknowledgements

Many thanks are due to Judith Paterson and Frances Ryan for efficient and thorough checking. Judith is Head of Advice and Rights at CPAG in Scotland; Frances is a welfare rights worker at CPAG in Scotland. Thanks also to Katherine Dawson for producing the index and Kathleen Armstrong for proofreading the text.

About Child Poverty Action Group

Child Poverty Action Group (CPAG) is a national charity that works on behalf of the nearly one in three children in the UK who are growing up in poverty. We use our understanding of what causes poverty and the impact it has on children's lives to campaign for policies that will prevent and solve poverty, for good.

Online, and through our books, training and advice services, CPAG provides trusted and expert information and advice for the welfare rights and advice community. Our advice lines support thousands of advisers a year, helping them give families the best information and advice. Our *Welfare Benefits and Tax Credits Handbook*, described as the 'adviser's bible', is used by Citizens Advice, local authorities and law centres throughout the UK. We also keep advisers up to date with trends and changes in the social security system through bulletins and our highly regarded training courses and seminars.

Poverty affects nearly one in three children in the UK today. When children grow up poor, they miss out, and so do the rest of us. They miss out on the things most children take for granted: warm clothes, school trips and having friends over for tea. They do less well at school and earn less money as adults. Any family can fall on hard times and find it difficult to make ends meet. But poverty is not inevitable. With the right policies every child can have the opportunity to do well in life, and we all share the rewards of having a stronger economy and a healthier, fairer society.

If you would like to join us to help end child poverty, please visit cpag.org.uk or follow us on Facebook (facebook.com/cpaguk) and Twitter (@cpaguk).

Keeping up to date

You can get the latest information on benefits by booking on a CPAG training course. We can also provide your workplace with in-house training. Our training courses are currently available online, so you can attend from wherever you are working. See cpag.org.uk/training for more information.

Our *Welfare Benefits and Tax Credits Handbook 2020/21*, published in April 2020, tells you all you need to know about entitlement to benefits and tax credits. Visit cpag.org.uk/shop to purchase a copy.

With up-to-date information, insights, decision-making tools and appeal-letter generators, AskCPAG is our online platform that supplements the expertise advisers have come to trust and rely on from our rights handbooks and training. AskCPAG provides digital access to our flagship *Welfare Benefits and Tax Credit Handbook*, which is fully searchable and updated throughout the year online. See askcpag.org.uk to subscribe or find out more.

Universal credit Early Warning System

CPAG's Early Warning System collects and analyses information about the impact of the roll-out of universal credit, as well as other changes in the benefits system. The cases we hear about inform our legal challenges, policy and campaign work. You can submit case studies or read our findings at cpag.org.uk/early-warning-system.

Getting advice

Your local Citizens Advice office or other advice centre can give you advice on benefits. See citizensadvice.org.uk and advicelocal.uk.

CPAG has a range of advice services for advisers.

For advisers in England, Wales and Northern Ireland:

Telephone: 020 7812 5231, Monday to Friday 10am to 12pm and 2pm to 4pm (for advice about any welfare benefit or tax credit matter).

Email: advice@cpag.org.uk (for enquiries about universal credit, child benefit and tax credits only).

Advisers supporting people living in London can get advice on universal credit by emailing UC-London@cpag.org.uk or by calling 020 7812 5221 (Wednesday 10am–12pm and 2pm–4pm).

For advisers in Scotland:

Telephone: 0141 552 0552, Monday to Thursday 10am to 4pm and Friday 10am to 12pm.

Email: advice@cpagscotland.org.uk.

For further information on CPAG's advice services, please visit cpag.org.uk/welfare-rights/advice-service or cpag.org.uk/scotland/welfare-rights/advice-line.

Contents

Chapter 1
What is universal credit

This chapter covers:

1. What is universal credit?

2. What is happening to the old benefits system?

3. How is universal credit administered?

4. How is universal credit different?

What you need to know

- Universal credit is a benefit for people of working age who are in or out of work. It has been gradually introduced for people making new claims throughout Great Britain since October 2013.

- Universal credit is administered by the Department for Work and Pensions and is claimed online.

- The amount of your universal credit depends on your income and savings – ie, it is 'means tested'. You do not need to have paid national insurance contributions to qualify.

- Other means-tested benefits and tax credits are being gradually replaced. Most claimants of these old benefits are due to be transferred to universal credit by 2023, although this might change.

1. What is universal credit?

Universal credit is a social security benefit for people of working age. It combines 'means-tested' support for adults, children and housing costs into one benefit.

The old means-tested benefits and tax credits for working-age people are being replaced by universal credit. This means that if you are, for example, a lone parent, sick or disabled, a carer, unemployed or in low-paid work, and you need help with your living expenses, the means-tested benefit you will claim is universal credit.

2. What is happening to the old benefits system?

Working-age 'means-tested benefits' and tax credits are being replaced by universal credit. However, there is a transition period of several years during which both systems will be in operation.

> Box A
> **Benefits and tax credits being replaced**
>
> The benefits and tax credits being replaced by universal credit are:
>
> - income support
> - income-based jobseeker's allowance
> - income-related employment and support allowance
> - housing benefit
> - child tax credit
> - working tax credit

You cannot usually make a new claim for the benefits and tax credits listed in Box A. The Department for Work and Pensions refers to these benefits and tax credits as 'legacy benefits'.

If you are already getting one of these old benefits or tax credits, you can continue to do so until you claim, or are transferred to, universal credit. The transfer process was due to take place for most claimants between 2020 and 2023, although that has been subject to delay and these dates may change. There is more information about transfers to universal credit in Chapter 2.

Box B
Which benefits remain?
- attendance allowance (or disability assistance in Scotland, when introduced)
- bereavement support payment
- carer's allowance (or carer's assistance in Scotland, when introduced)
- child benefit
- cold weather payments (or winter heating assistance in Scotland, when introduced)
- constant attendance allowance
- contribution-based jobseeker's allowance
- contributory employment and support allowance
- disability living allowance for children (or child disability payment in Scotland, when introduced)
- free school lunches
- funeral payments (or funeral support payment in Scotland)
- guardian's allowance
- Healthy Start vouchers (or Best Start foods in Scotland)
- help with health costs
- industrial injuries benefits (or employment-injury assistance in Scotland, when introduced)
- maternity allowance
- pension credit
- personal independence payment (or disability assistance in Scotland, when introduced)
- state pension
- school clothing grants
- Scottish child payment in Scotland, when introduced
- statutory adoption pay
- statutory maternity pay
- statutory paternity pay
- statutory shared parental pay and statutory shared parental bereavement pay
- statutory sick pay
- Sure Start maternity grant (or Best Start grant in Scotland)
- war disablement pension
- war widow's and widower's pension
- widowed parent's allowance
- winter fuel payment (or winter heating assistance in Scotland, when introduced)

Universal credit does not replace all the current benefits. You can still claim, or continue to get, the benefits in Box B after universal credit has been introduced.

3. How is universal credit administered?

The **Department for Work and Pensions (DWP)** is responsible for the administration of universal credit. The DWP also deals with the old out-of-work benefits that are being replaced and handles the transfer of these claims to universal credit. Different sections within the DWP deal with most of the other benefits that remain outside the universal credit system, but still interact with it. These include 'contributory benefits', pensions, and disability and carers' benefits.

HM Revenue and Customs (HMRC) administers tax credits, which are being replaced by universal credit. HMRC receives 'real-time information' on earnings from employers, which is then accessed by the DWP, so that universal credit payments can be automatically adjusted as people's earnings change. Child benefit and guardian's allowance remain the responsibility of HMRC.

Local authorities administer housing benefit, which is being replaced by universal credit. Existing claims continue until they are transferred to universal credit. Local authorities continue to deal with housing benefit for older people and for people in certain supported or temporary accommodation. They also keep their rent officers' functions in the private rented sector, and are responsible for council tax reduction schemes, discretionary housing payments, grants and other financial help.

Work coaches in local job centres oversee the 'work-related requirements' most people must meet in return for getting universal credit. There is more information about these in Chapter 6.

Citizens Advice has been funded by the government to provide a 'universal support' service since April 2019, offering people help to claim universal credit.

4. How is universal credit different?

There are a number of differences between universal credit and the old benefits and tax credits system.

- **Monthly assessment and payment periods.** Universal credit is assessed according to your circumstances over a month. Awards are based on your earnings and other income received in a month, and payment is made in one monthly sum. Under the old system, people usually get fortnightly payments of adult benefits and separate four-weekly payments of child tax credit. Because of this change, people claiming universal credit may be offered support with budgeting.

- **Online access.** Universal credit is claimed online. You manage your claim by signing into an online account. The Department for Work and Pensions (DWP) has worked with local authorities and Citizens Advice to provide more computers for people to use, more free online access and support to make a claim. The DWP may allow telephone access in limited circumstances and assistance in person in exceptional cases. There is no paper claim form.

- **No hours rules.** The old system has a variety of rules on the number of hours you can work. These make a difference to your entitlement and the amount of benefit you receive, depending on whether you or your partner work less or more than 16, 24 or 30 hours a week. Under universal credit, all work is permitted, encouraged and, in some cases, required, and earnings are automatically taken into account. Universal credit is designed to allow people to work a few hours a week. For example, unlike tax credits, you can get help with childcare costs in your universal credit, irrespective of how few hours you work.

- **Work incentives.** Universal credit was first introduced with a defining principle of 'making work pay', with work incentives that allow claimants to keep more of their universal credit as their earnings rise. For most claimants, this now means being better off by 37 pence for every £1 they earn. Some claimants get a 'work allowance' – an amount they can earn before their benefit is reduced in this way.

- **In-work conditionality.** Universal credit claimants who work part time may be obliged to look for more work. This is not a feature of the old working tax credit system, in which you can qualify if you work a certain number of hours. Universal credit claimants who do not do enough to increase their hours or pay can be given a 'sanction' (and the amount of their benefit is reduced).

Chapter 2
When universal credit affects you

This chapter covers:

1. When can you claim universal credit?

2. What happens if your circumstances change?

3. How do you transfer to universal credit?

What you need to know

- Universal credit is being introduced gradually. It has been introduced everywhere for people making new claims, but people already getting the old means-tested benefits and tax credits can stay on them (if they continue to be entitled) until they claim universal credit.

- Universal credit replaces the old means-tested benefits and tax credits for working-age people. In most cases, you cannot make a new claim for these benefits – you must claim universal credit instead. Once you have made a claim for universal credit, you can no longer get means-tested benefits or tax credits.

- If you are currently getting a means-tested benefit or tax credit, you can continue to do so for the time being. At some point, the Department for Work and Pensions will begin to stop some of these awards and will invite those affected to claim universal credit instead. This official transfer process was due to begin in 2020 and be completed by 2023 but is subject to delay.

- In some situations, you may transfer from the old means-tested benefits and tax credits system to universal credit before you are affected by the official transfer process – eg, if your circumstances change and you need to make a new claim for benefit.

1. When can you claim universal credit?

You can now claim universal credit in any area of Great Britain. In most cases, your personal circumstances are irrelevant. The main exception is for some severely disabled people; for more information, see below about how universal credit affects your other benefits and tax credits.

Before 12 December 2018, universal credit was introduced to different parts of the country on a rolling basis. In some areas, before 1 January 2018 you could only make a new claim for universal credit if you satisfied certain conditions, such as being single and not having children, not being sick or disabled, a carer or a student, and being a British citizen.

How does universal credit affect your other benefits and tax credits?

Universal credit replaces the means-tested benefits and tax credits for working-age people. In most cases, you cannot make a new claim for any of these benefits. There is an exception for some severely disabled people, although this exception is due to stop on 27 January 2021. If you are getting these benefits and then claim universal credit (eg, after a change in your circumstances), they stop. The means-tested benefits and tax credits being replaced by universal credit are:

- income support
- income-based jobseeker's allowance
- income-related employment and support allowance
- housing benefit (except for certain types of 'specified' and 'temporary' accommodation')
- child tax credit
- working tax credit

Under the universal credit system, contribution-based jobseeker's allowance is referred to as 'new-style' jobseeker's allowance and contributory employment and support allowance as 'new-style' employment and support allowance. Both these benefits depend on your national insurance contribution record. If your income is low enough, they can be topped up with universal credit.

Box A
Specified and temporary accommodation

'Specified accommodation' is accommodation where you can get certain types of help or support. It includes:

- accommodation provided by housing associations, charities and some councils where care, support or supervision is provided
- temporary accommodation for people who have left home because of domestic violence – sometimes called 'emergency' temporary accommodation

'Temporary accommodation' is homeless accommodation where you do not get care, support or supervision, and for which you pay rent to a local authority or a provider of social housing.

You can get child benefit, personal independence payment, disability living allowance and other non-means-tested benefits, including contribution-based jobseeker's allowance and contributory employment and support allowance, at the same time as universal credit. These benefits are not being replaced by universal credit.

EXAMPLE

Universal credit and means-tested benefits

Charlie is single and has one child, Sam, for whom he gets child benefit and child tax credit. Sam has a disability and gets disability living allowance. Charlie also gets income-related employment and support allowance and housing benefit, but he is not severely disabled. In December 2020, Charlie moves into private rented accommodation in a new local authority area, so his current housing benefit stops. Charlie cannot make a new claim for housing benefit (he does not live in specified or temporary accommodation, and is not severely disabled) and so claims universal credit. His awards of income-related employment and support allowance and child tax credit stop. He continues to get child benefit. Sam's disability living allowance also continues.

Box B
Pension credit

Pension credit is not being replaced by universal credit, but you cannot get pension credit and universal credit at the same time.

If you are in a couple and one of you is over pension age and one of you is under pension age, you can stay on pension credit if you already get it, but you cannot usually make a new claim for pension credit while your partner is under pension age, and you must claim universal credit instead. There is more about this in Chapter 10.

If you can get pension credit, you may also still be able to get child tax credit and working tax credit.

What CPAG says

Problems claiming 'new-style' jobseeker's allowance and employment and support allowance

You may be told that contribution-based jobseeker's allowance and contributory employment and support allowance no longer exist or that you cannot claim them under the universal credit system. That is incorrect. Universal credit only replaces *income-based* jobseeker's allowance and *income-related* employment and support allowance.

You can claim 'new-style' jobseeker's allowance online or, if you cannot claim online, by phoning 0800 055 6688 (textphone 0800 023 4888); or, if you cannot hear or speak on the phone, via Relay UK: 18001 then 0800 055 6688. See gov.uk/guidance/new-style-jobseekers-allowance. You can claim 'new-style' employment and support allowance online or, if you cannot claim online, by phoning 0800 328 5644 (textphone 0800 328 1344); or, if you cannot hear or speak on the phone, via Relay UK: 18001 then 1800 328 5644. See gov.uk/guidance/new-style-employment-and-support-allowance.

Who cannot claim universal credit?

Currently, some people cannot make a new claim for universal credit. They must claim the old 'means-tested benefits' and tax credits instead.

- From 16 January 2019 until 27 January 2021, if you or your partner count as severely disabled, meaning that you are entitled to a 'severe disability premium' in your means-tested benefit, you cannot claim universal credit. You remain on your old benefit (and can make a new claim for any of the other old means-tested benefits and tax credits) until you are affected by the official 'managed migration' process. (Seek advice as these dates may be subject to change.)

- If you are already getting either child tax credit or working tax credit, you can start to get the other – eg, if you are getting working tax credit and then have a child, you can get child tax credit. You do not *have* to claim universal credit instead, although you can if you want to make a claim.

- If you are living in 'specified' or 'temporary' accommodation, although you can claim universal credit for help with your living expenses, you must claim housing benefit for help with your rent and other housing costs.

2. What happens if your circumstances change?

In general, once you get universal credit you can remain entitled to it even though your circumstances change, provided you still satisfy the basic rules and financial conditions, such as being in Great Britain and having a low enough income. So, for instance, you can continue to get universal credit if you stop or start work, move house, or if you have a child or become ill.

Special rules apply, however, when you start or end a relationship. If you are getting universal credit as a single person but then become part of a couple, you should report this change to the Department for Work and Pensions (DWP). You can then get universal credit as a couple without having to make a new claim. If your partner was getting any of the old 'means-tested benefits' or tax credits, these stop. If s/he was getting pension credit, this also stops.

If you are getting universal credit as a couple but you then separate, you should report this change to the DWP. Both you and your ex-partner can remain on universal credit as single claimants without having to make new claims.

EXAMPLES

Change of circumstances

Peter has been getting universal credit as a single unemployed person. However, he becomes ill and is no longer fit for work. He is assessed as having limited capability for work and continues to receive universal credit on this basis. Although his universal credit does not increase, he no longer needs to look for work or be available for work.

Jane has been getting universal credit as a single parent. She meets Rosa and they become a couple. Rosa gets income-based jobseeker's allowance and housing benefit. They report the change to the offices handling their benefit claims. Jane and Rosa count as a couple for universal credit and they are treated as having made a joint claim. Rosa's income-based jobseeker's allowance and housing benefit now stop.

Roberto and Angela have been getting universal credit as a couple. When they split up, they tell the DWP. Both Roberto and Angela continue to receive universal credit as single people. They do not need to make new claims.

Reclaiming universal credit

If your entitlement to universal credit came to an end (eg, because your income was too high or you started studying), but you think you may be entitled again, you must make a new claim. If your entitlement ended because your income was too high, the DWP can treat you as having made a new claim for what would have been the next five of your monthly universal credit assessment periods. Check with the DWP if you are unsure if you need to reclaim.

In most cases, you cannot make a new claim for any of the old 'means-tested benefits' or tax credits instead.

If you reclaim universal credit within six months of your previous award ending, you should be able to log into your old universal credit online account and reclaim more quickly. There is more about this in Chapter 4.

EXAMPLE

Reclaiming universal credit

Ravinder was getting universal credit, but three months ago his award stopped when his earnings became too high. His earnings have gone down again and he wants to make another claim. Because it is less than six months since his previous award stopped, he can use his old online universal credit account to reclaim.

3. How do you transfer to universal credit?

At some point, you will transfer from the old 'means-tested benefits and tax credits system to universal credit. The Department for Work and Pensions (DWP) calls this 'migration' to universal credit.

There are two ways of migrating to universal credit.

- **'Natural migration'** to universal credit. In most cases, this happens when you are already getting one of the old means-tested benefits or tax credits, your circumstances change and you need to claim benefit, but you cannot make a new claim for one of the old means-tested benefits and tax credits and so you claim universal credit. That can happen at any time.

- **'Managed migration'** to universal credit. Under this official process, the DWP will notify you that your old benefit or tax credit is to end and that you will need to claim universal credit instead. You do not have a choice about your old benefit or tax credit ending. The DWP tested this process in a few cases and planned to migrate the remaining cases to universal credit between 2020 and 2023, but that has been subject to delay.

What CPAG says

Migration to universal credit

Some people on the old means-tested benefits and tax credits have been given incorrect official advice that they must claim universal credit, even when their circumstances have not changed and before they are affected by the managed migration process.

You do not need to claim universal credit if you do not want to, until either you are affected by the natural migration process following a change in your circumstances or the DWP notifies you that you are affected by the managed migration process.

Ask for an explanation for the advice you have been given. If you remain unhappy, consider making a complaint.

Some severely disabled people getting an old means-tested benefit have wrongly been allowed to claim and transfer to universal credit, when they should have been prevented from claiming universal credit and allowed to claim one or more of the means-tested benefits or tax credits instead. The DWP has been putting such people back on to their old means-tested benefits when requested, and the DWP agrees that it was a mistake to allow them to transfer to universal credit. If this applies to you, and you want to go back to your old means-tested benefit, contact the DWP.

Natural migration

You can usually claim universal credit whenever you want to. However, you are most likely to want to claim universal credit when there is a change in your circumstances that means you need to make a new claim for benefit, but you can no longer claim one of the old 'means-tested benefits' or tax credits. This is called 'natural migration' to universal credit.

Note: if you or your partner have a disability and are entitled to the 'severe disability premium' in your means-tested benefit (or have been entitled to it in the past month), from 16 January 2019 until 27 January 2021 you cannot make a new claim for universal credit until you are affected by the 'managed migration' process. Instead, you can make a new claim for the old means-tested benefits and tax credits. (Seek advice as these dates may be subject to change.)

Box C
When are you likely to migrate to universal credit?

- You have your first child – you cannot usually make a new claim for child tax credit unless you already get working tax credit.

- You move into a different local authority area and need help with your rent – you cannot usually make a new claim for housing benefit.

- You fail the 'work capability assessment' for employment and support allowance and choose to claim another benefit while the Department for Work and Pensions (DWP) considers your request for this to be looked at again – you cannot make a new claim for income-based jobseeker's allowance.

- You were working but become sick and cannot work for a while – you cannot make a new claim for income-related employment and support allowance.

Box D
When are you unlikely to migrate to universal credit?

- You are already getting child tax credit and have another child – no new claim for child tax credit is required.

- You are already getting working tax credit and have your first child – no new claim for child tax credit is required.

- You are already getting child tax credit and start work – no new claim for working tax credit is required.

- You move house but still pay rent in the same local authority area – no new claim for housing benefit is required.

- You fail the work capability assessment for employment and support allowance, but you choose not to claim benefit while the DWP reconsiders the decision and to wait until you have submitted your appeal, when you can then get paid employment and support allowance – no new claim for employment and support allowance is required.

Note: once you have transferred to universal credit via natural migration, you cannot usually return to the old means-tested benefits and tax credits, even if you stop being entitled to universal credit.

EXAMPLE

Natural migration

Pedro is unemployed and getting income-based jobseeker's allowance and housing benefit. He has heart problems, which make it difficult for him to continue looking for work, so he decides he wants to claim benefit on the basis of being too ill to work. Pedro does not have any children and is not entitled to the severe disability premium in his benefit. He cannot make a new claim for income-related employment and support allowance and so needs to claim universal credit instead. When he claims universal credit, his awards of income-based jobseeker's allowance and housing benefit stop. He has now transferred to universal credit via natural migration.

EXAMPLE

Natural migration

Gordon is disabled and entitled to the daily living component of personal independence payment, as well as income-related employment and support allowance and housing benefit, which include the severe disability premium. When Gordon moves into a new local authority area in December 2020, his housing benefit stops and he needs to make a new claim. Because he gets the severe disability premium, he cannot make a new claim for universal credit, and must make a new claim for housing benefit instead. Because he has not claimed universal credit, Gordon has not migrated to universal credit and his old means-tested benefits continue for now. (Note that this may be different from 27 January 2021, when severely disabled people are due to be no longer be prevented from making a claim for universal credit. This date was correct at the time this book was written.)

Are you worse off on universal credit?
When you migrate to universal credit, the amount of benefit you get is likely to change. Some people are better off (eg, if they are working and have childcare costs), but some people are worse off. In particular, you may be worse off on universal credit if you have a disability or if you have a disabled child. This is because (unlike the old 'means-tested benefits' and tax credits) universal credit does not include extra amounts specifically for disabled adults, and the amount for a disabled child is lower.

If you transfer to universal credit via 'natural migration', your universal credit does not include any 'transitional protection' to keep the amount of your benefit at the same level as you were getting before. So it is always best to get advice about whether you will be better or worse off on universal credit before claiming. Independent online benefit calculators are available at gov.uk/benefits-calculators.

If you were entitled to a 'severe disability premium' in your old benefit and you were correctly transferred to universal credit by natural migration, you may be entitled to an extra amount of universal credit. For example, you may have been correctly transferred because at the time of the transfer your old benefit did not include the premium, but the premium was later backdated to before you transferred. The DWP calls this a 'transitional SDP amount'. If you were entitled to the premium at the time you claimed universal credit but were wrongly allowed to proceed with the claim, the DWP may agree to put you back on your old means-tested benefit.

A severe disability premium was included in your (or your partner's) means-tested benefit if you (or your partner) were getting a qualifying disability benefit (such as the 'daily living component' of personal independence payment), no one got carer's allowance for looking after you, and you technically counted as living alone. Chapter 5 has more information on the amount of your universal credit, including the transitional SDP amount.

What CPAG says

No one worse off on universal credit?

The government had stated that no one would be worse off on universal credit. It promised transitional protection so that people entitled to a higher amount under the old benefits and tax credits system would not lose out in cash terms when they transferred to universal credit. However, this will only apply to people who are transferred to universal credit under the official 'managed migration' process.

In general, there is no transitional protection for people who transfer to universal credit under natural migration when their circumstances change – eg, after moving to a new local authority area, the birth of a child, bereavement or relationship breakdown. As you may be worse off on universal credit, get advice before making a claim. Once you have transferred, you cannot usually change your mind and return to the old means-tested benefits and tax credits.

Following legal challenges in court, the transitional SDP amount was introduced for severely disabled people who were worse off after transferring to universal credit. However, this transitional SDP amount may not bring the universal credit up to the level of the old means-tested benefit in all cases. Cases continue to come before the courts regarding the lack of full transitional protection for severely disabled people and others – for example, those who wrongly had their old means-tested benefit terminated by the DWP and then decided to claim universal credit and found themselves worse off.

Managed migration

In 2019, the Department for Work and Pensions (DWP) began testing the transferral of a small group of people getting the old 'means-tested benefits' and tax credits to universal credit. This process was due to be extended to all other people getting the old means-tested benefits and tax credits between 2020 and 2023. The process of bringing your entitlement to means-tested benefits and tax credits to an end and allowing you to make a new claim for universal credit is called 'managed migration'. However, the test and the extension of the test to all other people was delayed due to the coronavirus pandemic, and these dates are now subject to change. What follows is what was known about the process at the time this book was updated in July 2020.

When the process begins (in most cases this is unlikely to be before 2021), the DWP will write to you, notifying you of when you will be affected. Until then, you cannot transfer to universal credit by this process.

The DWP starts the process by sending you a 'migration notice', informing you that your old means-tested benefits and tax credits awards are to end (on your 'migration day') and that you will need to make a claim for universal credit instead. When you are sent the migration notice, you become a 'notified person'.

You are given a date by when you must make your universal credit claim (your 'deadline day'). This must be at least three months from the date of your migration notice. You can be given longer to claim universal credit if the DWP agrees you have a good reason – eg, if you are unwell or need to arrange for help to make your claim.

Your entitlement to the old means-tested benefits and tax credits ends when you claim universal credit or, if you do not claim, on the day before your deadline day. As long as you claim universal credit within a month of your deadline day (your 'final deadline'), you can still get universal credit under this process. However, the DWP is likely to require you to have made a successful claim for universal credit. This means you must verify your identity and attend an interview after you have submitted your online claim form. If you do not do so, the DWP will refuse you universal credit. More information about this is in Chapter 4.

You are not automatically entitled to universal credit – you must still satisfy the usual rules of entitlement. These are explained in Chapter 3. However, if you are a student when your old means-tested benefits and tax credits end, you can get universal credit, even if you do not satisfy the rule about not 'receiving education'. If you transfer from tax credits, any capital you have over £16,000 is ignored for one year.

Some people are better off on universal credit. If you will be worse off after transferring via managed migration, you are entitled to a top-up amount of universal credit (called a 'transitional element') so you do not lose out. For more on the transitional element and how it is calculated, see Chapter 5.

What CPAG says

Managed migration

When it is introduced, there will be no choice about being affected by the managed migration process. Even if you do not claim universal credit, your old means-tested benefits will stop. It is therefore extremely unlikely that refusing to claim universal credit by the date you are given will be in your best interests.

If you are notified that you are affected by the managed migration process, but need more time to claim universal credit (eg, because you are unwell or need help to claim), contact the DWP and explain why you need more time.

If you will be worse off on universal credit, your benefit should include a transitional element, provided you claim universal credit within the time allowed and you are then entitled to universal credit. If you claim later, you have not transferred to universal credit under the managed migration process and are not entitled to any transitional protection.

Chapter 3
Who can get universal credit

This chapter covers:

1. Who can get universal credit?

2. What are the basic rules?

3. What are the financial conditions?

4. Can you get any other financial help?

What you need to know

- To get universal credit, you must meet the basic rules of entitlement and the financial conditions.

- There are basic rules about your age, residence in Great Britain, whether you are in education and about agreeing to a 'claimant commitment'. This lists what you must do in return for receiving universal credit.

- The financial conditions are about your income and capital (such as savings, investments and certain types of property). You cannot get universal credit if your capital is above £16,000 (although some capital is ignored).

- If you are in a couple, both of you must usually meet the basic rules and the financial conditions.

1. Who can get universal credit?

Universal credit is a benefit for both single people and couples on a low income to provide financial support for living costs, children, housing costs and other needs. You can get universal credit if you are in or out of work.

You can get universal credit if you meet the basic rules of entitlement and the financial conditions. Provided you meet these, you can get universal credit regardless of your particular circumstances. For example, you can claim if you are:

- a parent, including a lone parent
- ill or disabled
- a carer
- unemployed
- employed or self-employed

Note: in the period from 16 January 2019 to 26 January 2021 inclusive, some people who are getting a benefit that includes a 'severe disability premium' cannot make a new claim for universal credit. This chapter does not cover when you can claim universal credit – it explains the general rules on who can get universal credit once you are able to make a claim. Chapter 2 has more information on when you can claim universal credit.

> **EXAMPLES**
>
> **Who can get universal credit**
>
> George has been made redundant. Depending on his income and his other circumstances, he can get universal credit to provide him with some financial help.
>
> Rosie is a lone parent working 12 hours a week in a low-paid job. She has two children and they live in a housing association property. She can claim universal credit to provide her with some financial help.

Your specific circumstances are taken into account to decide how much universal credit you get and what you are expected to do to move towards work. There is more information in Chapter 5 on the amount of universal credit you can get, and in Chapter 6 on the 'work-related requirements' you may need to satisfy.

Couples

If you are in a couple, you normally make a joint claim with your partner. Both of you must usually satisfy the basic rules of entitlement and the financial conditions.

You count as a member of a couple if you are living together and are married or civil partners, or if you are living together as if you were a married couple. In some circumstances, you must claim as a single person, even though you are in a couple – eg, if your partner is under 18, but you are not. Chapter 4 contains some examples and more information about claiming universal credit.

In two circumstances, it is possible to get universal credit as a couple even though one of you does not meet the basic rules. These are if one of you has reached pension age and the other has not, or if one of you is a student and the other is not.

EXAMPLE

One member of a couple is a student

Molly is on a full-time undergraduate course and her partner Mike is unemployed. They have no children. They can claim universal credit as a couple, even though Molly is a student.

If you are in a couple and your partner has not accepted a 'claimant commitment' outlining what you must do in order to receive universal credit, but you have, you cannot get universal credit. You must each accept your own claimant commitment to qualify. Chapter 6 has more information about the claimant commitment.

Who cannot get universal credit?

Because universal credit is being introduced gradually, some people with a disability cannot currently make a new claim for universal credit and must claim the old 'means-tested benefits' and tax credits instead. Chapter 2 has more information on this.

If you are in prison, you can get universal credit for up to six months – but only for your housing costs, and only if you were getting universal credit, including for housing costs, before going into prison. You must not be likely to be in prison for more than six months.

You cannot get universal credit if you are fully maintained by a religious order.

EXAMPLE

Who cannot get universal credit

John is sentenced to 18 months in prison. He was getting universal credit that included an amount for his housing costs before he went in, but cannot continue to receive this because he is likely to be in prison for more than six months. If he were likely to be released within six months, he could get universal credit for his housing costs for the first six months.

---

2. What are the basic rules?

To be entitled to universal credit, you must meet certain basic rules. There are some exceptions, which are explained in this section.

EXAMPLE

The basic rules

Jane and Kevin are a British couple, both aged 20. They are not students. Can they claim universal credit?

They meet the age rules, they are in Great Britain and they are not in education, so they can claim universal credit. They must claim jointly as a couple. They must also meet the financial conditions and agree to meet certain work-related requirements. Their income will be compared with the maximum amount of universal credit for their circumstances to see whether they get an award and, if so, how much this will be.

You meet the basic rules for universal credit if:

- you are aged 18 or over
- you are under pension age
- you are not in education
- you are resident in Great Britain
- you accept a 'claimant commitment'

Are you under 18?

Usually, you must be aged 18 or over to claim universal credit. You can claim at age 16 or 17 (including if you are studying) if:

- you have a child
- you have a disability and get disability living allowance or personal independence payment and you are assessed as having 'limited capability for work'
- you are 'without parental support'

Box A
Without parental support

You are 'without parental support' if you are living away from your parents (or someone acting in their place) because you are estranged from them or because there is a risk to your health or if your parents cannot support you because they are ill, disabled, in prison or not allowed to enter Great Britain, or you are an orphan. This does not apply to you if you are looked after by the local authority, or someone else (such as a grandparent) is acting in place of a parent.

Note: if you claim universal credit for yourself, your parent cannot continue to claim benefit for you, so it may be important to check this before you claim.

Provided you are not a student, you can also get universal credit when you are 16 or 17 under certain circumstances.

- You have given birth within the last 15 weeks, or you are pregnant and your baby is due within 11 weeks.

- You are ill or disabled and have limited capability for work or you are waiting for a limited capability for work assessment and have provided a 'fit note' from your doctor.
- You are a carer – usually, you must also get carer's allowance.

If you are a care leaver aged 16 or 17, you can only get universal credit if you have a child, or if you are ill or disabled. Your universal credit does not include an amount for your housing costs.

Are you over pension age?

To get universal credit as a single person, you must be below pension age. Pension age is now the same for both men and women and is gradually increasing from age 65 for new claimants so as to reach 66 by October 2020. Between 2026 and 2028 it will rise to 67.

If you are getting universal credit and form a couple with someone over pension age, you can no longer claim pension credit but must usually claim universal credit instead (you cannot get both universal credit and pension credit). There is more information about this in Chapter 10.

EXAMPLE

One member of a couple is over pension age

Joan is 58 and gets universal credit. In June 2021 she moves in with her partner Charlie, who is 66 and gets an occupational pension. They claim universal credit as a couple.

Joan must meet work-related requirements as a condition of getting universal credit, but Charlie does not need to.

Are you a student?

In general, you cannot get universal credit if you are a student. This is called 'receiving education' by the Department for Work and Pensions (DWP). However, there are some exceptions.

Box B
Who is a student?

- From your 16th birthday to 1 September after your 19th birthday, you are a student if you are at school or college on a non-advanced course (eg, below degree or Higher National Certificate level), or you are in training that is 'approved' by the DWP.

- You are a student while you are on a full-time course of advanced education – eg, at Higher National Certificate level or above.

- You are a student while you are on another kind of full-time course, either advanced or non-advanced, if you get a loan or grant for your maintenance.

- Even if you are not in one of the above three groups, you count as a student if your course is not compatible with the hours that you are expected to be looking for work or with any other 'work-related requirements' you are expected to meet for your universal credit claim.

Which students can get universal credit?

You can get universal credit while you are student if you are in one of the following groups.

- You have a child.

- You are a single foster parent (including some kinship carers).

- You are a foster parent and your partner is also a full-time student.

- You are disabled and get disability living allowance or personal independence payment and you have been assessed as having 'limited capability for work'.

- You are aged under 22, without parental support, and on a non-advanced course which you started before your 21st birthday.

- You are a member of a couple and your partner is not a student, or your partner is a student but would be eligible for universal credit her/himself while studying.

- You have taken time out from your course because of illness or caring responsibilities, you have now recovered or your caring responsibilities have now ended, and you are waiting to rejoin your course.

- You are over pension age.

How much universal credit you get, if any, depends on your income. Student loans and some grants count as income, but usually only during the academic year. Chapter 5 explains how your universal credit is worked out.

What CPAG says

Problems with student claims

If you are a student and are in one of the above groups, but you are told you cannot get universal credit, ask for a 'mandatory reconsideration' of this decision. As long as you meet one of the above conditions, you are eligible for universal credit, even though you are a student. The DWP sometimes gets this wrong and assumes you cannot get universal credit if you are studying.

EXAMPLES

Students who can get universal credit

Graham is on a full-time advanced course. He is disabled and gets personal independence payment. He gets contributory employment and support allowance and has been assessed as having limited capability for work. He can claim universal credit.

Lauren is on a full-time advanced course and is a lone parent. She can claim universal credit.

Residence in Great Britain

In general, you must be resident in Great Britain to claim universal credit, although there are exceptions to this.

Are you going abroad?

You can continue to get universal credit while abroad for up to one month. You must usually continue to meet your 'work-related requirements'. There are only limited circumstances when you can get universal credit for longer than this – eg, for up to two months if a close relative has died or for up to six months if the trip is to get medical treatment. If you stay at home and your partner is abroad for longer than a month, the amount of your universal credit usually decreases, so it is important to tell the Department for Work and Pensions (DWP). Some people who work abroad can get universal credit – eg, members of the armed forces.

Coronavirus

During the coronavirus pandemic, problems have arisen where claimants are abroad and have been unable to return to Great Britain – eg, if you are in a couple you may be in Great Britain but your partner has been abroad for more than a month because s/he is unable to travel back. Normal rules would enable you still to get universal credit at a decreased amount – ie, as a single person. In practice, if the problem has been due to coronavirus, the DWP may be willing to adopt a more flexible approach, although the rules have not been changed.

Have you come to Great Britain from abroad?

In some cases, if you have come from abroad you cannot get universal credit, even though you are resident in Great Britain.

You cannot usually get universal credit if you are defined as a 'person subject to immigration control'. You will usually have 'no recourse to public funds' stamped in your passport or stated in the document issued to you confirming your leave to remain. This means you cannot claim most social security benefits, including universal credit. People who have refugee leave, humanitarian protection or discretionary leave, and those in some other circumstances, can get universal credit.

You must have a 'right to reside' in Great Britain. If you are a UK national, you have a right to reside. The requirement to have a right to reside has mostly affected European nationals. Following the UK leaving the European Union (EU), during the 'transition' (or implementation) period, which is currently due to end on 31 December 2020, if you are from a country in the European Economic Area and are working or self-employed, you usually have a right to reside. There are other circumstances in which you may also have a right to reside, but being a jobseeker on its own is not sufficient for universal credit. If you began residing in the UK before the end of the transition period, you may also have a right to reside under the EU Settlement Scheme, but this will only count for universal credit purposes if you have 'settled' status under that scheme ('pre-settled' status will not count for universal credit).

At the end of the transition period, these rules will be different, and if you are from the European Economic Area and come to live in the UK after the end of the transition period, you will not be able to apply to the EU Settlement Scheme. Instead, you will have to satisfy new rules that are likely to be the same as those for people coming to the UK from outside Europe. However, the details of these new rules were not known at the time this book was updated.

EXAMPLES

Right to reside – before the end of the 'transition' period (currently set for 31 December 2020)

Natasha is French and a lone parent. She is working full time in Great Britain. She has a right to reside as a worker and can claim universal credit.

Saskia is Lithuanian and a lone parent of a six-month-old baby. She is a full-time student but has never worked in Britain. She has applied to the EU Settlement Scheme and been given pre-settled status, but this does not count for universal credit and so she is not entitled to it.

You may also have to be 'habitually resident' before you can get universal credit. In broad terms, this means that you have been living here for a while and intend to stay for some time to come.

Accepting a claimant commitment

To be entitled to universal credit, you must usually accept a 'claimant commitment'. This sets out what you must do to receive your universal credit award. The key part of a claimant commitment is about your 'work-related requirements'. There is more information about the claimant commitment in Chapter 6.

3. What are the financial conditions?

To be entitled to universal credit, your income must be sufficiently low. How much income you can have and still be entitled to some universal credit depends on your circumstances. Usually, as your income increases, the amount of universal credit you get decreases. If you have a partner, it is your combined income that counts.

Your capital (eg, savings and investments) must not be more than £16,000. If it is higher than £16,000, you are not entitled to universal credit. If you have a partner, it is your combined capital that counts. **Note:** capital over £16,000 is expected to be disregarded for 12 months if you are transferred to universal credit from tax credits under the 'managed migration' process.

There is more information about the income and capital rules in Chapter 5.

You must also meet the basic rules.

4. Can you get any other financial help?

If you get universal credit, you may be eligible for the following.

- A Sure Start maternity grant. This is a grant (£500 in 2020/21) to help with the costs of a newborn baby, usually only if there is no other child younger than 16 in your family. In Scotland, you are eligible for a Best Start grant instead.

- Help with council tax if you are on a low income. Apply to your local council tax reduction scheme.

- A funeral expenses payment to cover basic funeral costs. In Scotland, you are eligible for funeral support payment instead.

- A cold weather payment for weeks when the temperature is below freezing (or winter heating assistance in Scotland, when introduced).

- Healthy Start vouchers (for milk, fruit and vegetables) and vitamins if you are pregnant or have a young child. In Scotland, you may be eligible for a Best Start foods payment instead.

- Free prescriptions, NHS sight tests, vouchers for glasses, dental treatment and fares to hospital. You are only eligible if your monthly earnings are no more than £435, or £935 if you have a child or get an element for 'limited capability for work' or 'limited capability for work-related activity' in your universal credit award. **Note:** prescriptions are free for everyone in Wales and Scotland, and NHS sight tests are free for everyone in Scotland.

Under the old benefits system, if you get certain 'means-tested benefits', such as income support, income-based jobseeker's allowance, income-related employment and support allowance or child tax credit, you qualify for other financial help. Universal credit may also help you qualify for such help. This is known as 'passporting'. You may also have to have earnings below a certain amount to qualify.

Other financial help includes:

- free school lunches (in primary school for at least the first three years and on the basis of 'passporting' thereafter)
- school clothing grants
- help with heating and energy efficiency measures
- legal aid
- local leisure facility discounts
- social tariffs from utility companies

Some schemes are administered by central government departments, some by the Scottish and Welsh governments, and some by local authorities or other agencies. Some of this passported help is provided in cash or vouchers, and some as discounts on charges.

In general, you must make a separate claim for the passported help. In some cases, you must receive the necessary out-of-work benefit to qualify, and people not getting the required benefit but who are on a low income are excluded. As universal credit is introduced and these means-tested benefits are abolished, the existing criteria will change, but the government intends that people who would have qualified under the old system remain eligible.

Further information

There is more information about who can get universal credit and the other benefits you may qualify for in CPAG's *Welfare Benefits and Tax Credits Handbook*.
There is more information about benefits for students in CPAG's *Student Support and Benefits Handbook* and CPAG in Scotland's *Benefits for Students in Scotland Handbook*.

Chapter 4
Claiming universal credit

This chapter covers:

1. Who should claim universal credit?

2. How do you make a claim?

3. When should you claim?

4. How are you paid?

5. What happens if your circumstances change?

What you need to know

- Couples make a joint claim for universal credit. If you are a lone parent or a single person, you make a single claim. The usual way to claim is online.

- Universal credit is normally paid directly into your bank account. Couples may have a joint account or can choose which partner should be paid.

- Payments are usually made monthly. There are alternative arrangements if you are in exceptional circumstances and need help managing your money. If you live in Scotland, you can ask to be paid fortnightly.

- Unless you are told otherwise, you do not need to report changes in your earnings, but you must report any other changes in your circumstances.

1. Who should claim universal credit?

Universal credit is a benefit to provide support for adults and children. If you are single or a lone parent, you claim for yourself as a single person. If you are in a couple, you make a joint claim. However, if you are in a couple and one of you does not meet the basic rules for universal credit (eg, if s/he is abroad or away from home for an extended period, or if s/he is under 18), you cannot make a joint claim: you must claim as a single person. It is important to give details about both of you when you claim, because even though you do not get an amount for your partner in your award, you are usually still treated as a couple for other parts of the assessment. So, for example, your joint income and capital are taken into account, and your partner's circumstances count when deciding whether you can get any help with childcare costs.

EXAMPLES

Claiming universal credit

Eva is 17 and lives with her partner Ryan, who is 18 and looking for work. Ryan claims universal credit as a single person because Eva is not entitled as a 17 year old. His standard allowance is the amount for a single person.

Theo is 19. He lives with his 17-year-old partner Johanna and their baby. Because Johanna has a child and so is entitled to universal credit as a 17 year old, they can make a joint claim.

If you have been claiming universal credit jointly as a couple but have now separated from your partner, tell the Department for Work and Pensions (DWP). You can both stay on universal credit as single people without having to make new claims.

If you become a couple (eg, you and your partner start living together), you do not need to make a new claim if one or both of you is already getting universal credit. Tell the DWP about the change in your situation and provide any information required. If one partner was getting 'means-tested benefits' or tax credits, tell the DWP or Tax Credit Office. You cannot get the old means-tested benefits and tax credits at the same time as universal credit, so these will stop. There is more about this in Chapter 2.

2. How do you make a claim?

You must claim universal credit online at gov.uk/apply-universal-credit. Call the free universal credit helpline if you need help with this (Monday to Friday 8am to 6pm: 0800 328 5644; textphone 0800 328 1344; Welsh language 0800 328 1744; or if you cannot hear or speak on the phone Relay UK: 18001 then 0800 328 5644).

Box A

Information you need to complete the online claim form

When you are ready to claim, make sure you have the following information to hand:

- your email address
- your mobile phone number
- your national insurance number
- details of the people who live with you, such as your partner, children or lodgers
- any child benefit reference numbers
- details of any income, such as payslips or other benefits
- any savings or capital, such as shares or property that you rent to others
- your rent agreement
- details and registration number of your childcare provider
- details of the bank account you want your universal credit paid into – either your own account or a joint account with your partner
- verification of your identity, such as a debit or credit card, a recent bank statement, driving licence or passport

---

After you submit your claim, you are given a phone number to book an appointment for an interview at your local job centre. Couples must both attend.

At the interview, you are asked to confirm your identity and sign a copy of your claim details. You will meet your 'work coach' and agree what you will do next to look for or prepare for work. This goes into your 'claimant commitment', which is a record of what you are expected to do. You must sign this, otherwise your claim will be refused. There is more information about your 'work-related requirements' in Chapter 6.

Box B
Completing your online claim form

- Completing the claim is likely to take up to 40 minutes.

- First, you are asked to set up an online account by entering a username, password and answering two security questions. You must also give your email address.

- If you do not have all the information you need to make the claim, you can log in again at any time during the next 28 days to complete the form, but your date of claim will only be from the date you submit your completed form.

- You are asked to verify your identity online. If you cannot manage this, log into your online account later and complete and submit your claim. Your identity can be verified at the job centre instead. You should be given at least a month to arrange and attend the interview at the job centre.

- If you are claiming as a couple, both you and your partner must make an online claim. The first person to claim is given a 'linking code' to give to her/his partner, so that the two claims can be linked together as one.

- When you get to the end of your online claim, you are given a summary of the information you have entered. You have a chance to go back and correct any mistakes. When you are happy that the information is correct, submit your claim.

Coronavirus

During the coronavirus pandemic, claims for universal credit increased greatly and waiting times for getting on to the website and getting a response from the helpline all increased. But no rules have been introduced allowing claims to be backdated because of these problems. Job centres have been temporarily closed and interviews at job centres have not been taking place. Where this applies, you may be asked instead to submit more evidence online and to take part in an interview by telephone.

What CPAG says

Making a successful claim

It can be difficult to get through all the stages of the universal credit claims process. As well as submitting an online claim, you must verify your identity, either online or in person at the job centre, and first book and then attend an interview to agree a claimant commitment. If you miss any of these stages, your claim will be 'closed' and you are not paid.

- Ask for help if you have any difficulty with your claim. Call the free universal credit helpline (Monday to Friday 8am to 6pm: 0800 328 5644; textphone 0800 328 1344; Welsh language 0800 328 1744) or contact your local job centre. You can find the address and phone number of your local job centre at gov.uk/contact-jobcentre-plus. Also, your local Citizens Advice office should be able to help you make your claim. You can find details in the phone book, local library, via citizensadvice.org.uk or, if you live in Scotland, via cas.org.uk.

- If you are helping someone to claim, remember that many people also need help to book and attend their job centre interview. A third of people who manage to submit an online claim find their claim is closed because they do not book or attend the interview.

- If your claim is 'closed', make a new claim as soon as you can. Ask for the new claim to be backdated if any difficulty you had was connected to a disability or ill health. Ask for compensation if the DWP gave you the wrong advice or made it hard for you to get through the process.

- If the DWP 'closes' your claim, it has made a decision that you are not entitled to universal credit. You can appeal against this. First ask for a 'mandatory reconsideration' of the decision. You can do this online, or by phone if your online journal has been removed.

You receive a text or email in your online journal when the decision on your universal credit claim is available. This gives details of how the amount of your award has been worked out, including which 'elements' are included and any deductions for earnings and income. The decision tells you about your appeal rights.

Are you unable to claim online?

If you do not have online access at home or you are unable to use the internet, your local job centre may be able to help you or direct you to local organisations that can help you make your claim. Your local Citizens Advice Bureau should have a 'Help to Claim' service where you can get help in making your claim and getting your first payment.

If you cannot claim online, you may be allowed to claim by telephone. A Department for Work and Pensions (DWP) employee takes your details and completes an online claim for you. If you cannot use the telephone, you can ask to claim in person – eg, at a local office or by the DWP visiting you at home. However, this is intended to be only for people with exceptional circumstances and so may not be agreed. If you claim by phone or in person, your claim starts when you first contact the DWP to say you want to claim, so it is important to do so quickly if you cannot claim online.

There is no paper claim form for universal credit.

If you cannot make a claim or act on your own behalf, perhaps because you have a mental health problem or learning disability, someone else (called an 'appointee') can be authorised to act on your behalf. This could be a friend or relative. The appointee not only makes the claim but also takes on your responsibilities as a claimant, such as reporting any changes in your circumstances.

Have you claimed universal credit before?

If you were getting universal credit in the past and your previous claim ended within the last six months, you can log into your previous online account to reclaim. Your new claim takes less time than your earlier one. You are paid on the same dates as before.

If you are reclaiming universal credit because your job has ended, try to restart your claim within seven days of the job ending, to ensure your first payment is backdated as far as possible. If you cannot do so and you have a good reason for the delay, your first payment will still be for the maximum amount.

Coronavirus

Under rules introduced during the coronavirus pandemic, if you have claimed universal credit before and, because your income was too high, that claim was refused or your award of universal credit was stopped, you can be automatically treated as claiming again during the following five monthly assessment periods that would have applied had you been awarded universal credit. If that applies to you, you are treated as claiming again during each of those five monthly periods, without you actually making a claim. This may help you if, having been refused universal credit or had your award stopped because your income was too high, your income decreases at some point in the following five months, and the Department of Work and Pensions (DWP) is aware of that decrease. These rules may be changed or removed at some point. Check with the DWP if you are unsure whether you need to reclaim.

3. When should you claim?

Usually, your entitlement to universal credit starts when you submit your claim, so it is important not to delay – claim as soon as you think you may be entitled. However, it is sometimes possible for a claim to be backdated.

When can your claim be backdated?

Your claim can only be backdated in certain circumstances and for a maximum of one month. If any of the following apply to you and mean that you could not have reasonably claimed earlier, ask the Department for Work and Pensions (DWP) to backdate your claim for up to a month. Note that no specific rules have been made allowing backdating due to problems during the coronavirus pandemic.

- You have a disability.

- You send a medical certificate to say that you could not claim earlier because you were ill.

- You were getting jobseeker's allowance or employment and support allowance which ended, but you were only notified after it ended.

- You could not claim online because the system was not working.

- You were in a couple, but are now claiming as a single person and your former partner did not accept a 'claimant commitment', which meant that your joint claim was refused or stopped.

If you are a couple claiming universal credit jointly, both of you must be in one of these circumstances.

EXAMPLES

Backdating a claim

Amina is 20 and has just had her first baby. She is a lone parent. A week after the baby is born, she completes the online claim for universal credit. Her award is not backdated and she misses out on a week's money.

Darius has been in hospital after having a heart attack. He is self-employed and has not been able to work for three weeks. When he gets home, he claims universal credit. He asks for it to be backdated and sends in his medical certificate. The DWP accepts that it was not reasonable for him to have claimed earlier and backdates his award.

> **EXAMPLE**
>
> **Backdating a claim**
>
> Joe lost his job on Monday. He needs help to make an online claim for universal credit. As he has no computer himself and is not confident about using one, on Saturday he goes to his daughter's house and with her help submits his online claim. His award is not backdated.
>
> If Joe had telephoned the DWP to ask to claim by phone, his award could have started from the date of the call.

4. How are you paid?

Universal credit is paid directly into your bank or building society account in monthly payments. It is paid in arrears.

You must wait for one month and up to another seven days from the date you claim before you get your first payment. You are then paid on the same date each month. If this falls at a weekend or on a bank holiday, you are paid on the last working day before that. The amount you get does not change with the number of days in the month.

Each payment is based on your circumstances in the last monthly 'assessment period'. This is one calendar month, beginning with the first day of your entitlement to universal credit.

> **EXAMPLE**
>
> **When you are paid**
>
> Keith is unemployed. He claims universal credit on 11 October. His first monthly assessment period starts on 11 October and ends on 10 November. He gets his first monthly payment of universal credit paid into his bank account seven days later on 17 November and on the 17th of each month after that.

If you are in a couple and claiming jointly, all your univ
usually paid to one of you. It is up to you to decide wh
it is paid into, or you can have a joint account. If you c
the Department for Work and Pensions (DWP) can mak

If your partner will not let you have any of the money, you ca.
the DWP to split the monthly payments between you, or pay them
to you. The DWP must decide that it is in your, or your child's,
interest to be paid in this way. These 'alternative payment
arrangements' are meant to be exceptional to avoid hardship – eg,
if there is domestic violence or if your partner is not managing the
household finances properly.

Can you manage until your first payment?

It will be at least five weeks from submitting your claim before
you are paid. Sometimes, the wait is much longer. At your initial
interview at the job centre, you are asked whether you can manage
until your first universal credit payment, and you may be offered a
'universal credit advance' to help tide you over. The advance is up to
a full month's payment. You pay it back out of your universal credit
award, which can mean large reductions in your payments for up to
12 months.

If, after your initial interview, you decide that you need an advance,
you can apply through your online account or by phoning the
universal credit helpline (Monday to Friday 8am to 6pm: 0800 328
5644; textphone 0800 328 1344; Welsh language 0800 328 1744; or
if you cannot hear or speak on the phone Relay UK: 18001 then
0800 328 5644). You should apply before the end of the first
'assessment period'.

You can also ask for an advance while you wait for the amount of
your universal credit award to increase after your circumstances
change – eg, after you leave a job.

The Department for Work and Pensions (DWP) only gives you
an advance if it considers you are in financial need – eg, if you
cannot afford to pay your gas or electricity bills and are not
owed any wages.

You cannot appeal if the DWP refuses to give you an advance or about the amount of your repayments. If you are refused an advance, provide more information about your situation and ask the DWP to reconsider its decision.

EXAMPLE

Universal credit advance

Carmine is a lone parent with one child. She works part time and rents her home. Carmine claims universal credit. Her part-time wages are not enough to buy food and pay the bills. At her job centre interview, she asks for a universal credit advance to help her manage until her first payment. Her request is accepted and an advance of £1,200 is paid into her bank account five days later, estimated to be her full monthly award. Five weeks later, she receives her first monthly universal credit payment. She gets £1,073 a month because £127 is taken off each month to repay the advance.

You may be able to get help in a crisis from your local authority's local welfare assistance scheme.

Are monthly payments causing problems?

When you claim universal credit, you are offered advice about budgeting. This may be online, by telephone or in person at a local money advice service.

If the way you are paid is causing you difficulty, you can ask to be paid in a different way. Phone 0800 328 5644 or ask your 'work coach' at the job centre about 'alternative payment arrangements'.

If you are accepted as eligible, there are three main alternative payment arrangements.

- You can be paid twice a month or, very exceptionally, four times a month.

- Your rent can be paid directly to your landlord.

- Your payment can be split between you and your partner.

The Department for Work and Pensions (DWP) decides whether you can be paid in one of the alternative ways. You cannot appeal if you disagree, but you can give more information about your situation and ask the DWP to reconsider. The decision is based on guidance and depends on your circumstances. The DWP reviews the arrangements after a period of time, usually from three months to two years.

If you live in Scotland and do not already have alternative payment arrangements in place, you can choose to be paid twice a month, and choose to have your rent paid directly to your landlord (called 'Scottish choices'). You do not have to be accepted as eligible.

Box C

Alternative payment arrangements

You are most likely to be accepted for an alternative payment arrangement if:

- you have rent arrears or are threatened with eviction or repossession
- you have severe debt problems
- you have difficulty reading or writing, or with simple maths
- you have a learning disability or a mental health condition
- you have an alcohol, drug or gambling addiction
- you are under 18 or a care leaver
- you are homeless, or in temporary or supported accommodation
- you are (or were) experiencing domestic violence
- you are a family with multiple or complex needs

There are other reasons given in the government's guidance why someone might have difficulty managing, so it is worth explaining why you need this help.

What CPAG says

Avoiding rent arrears

You may find that you have built up rent arrears – either as a result of having to wait for your first payment of universal credit, or because the 'housing costs element' for your rent is not paid directly to your landlord. The following may help you avoid rent arrears.

- When you make your claim, make sure you report all the details of your rent. Remember that you are still liable to pay your rent. If you did not report your housing costs at first, ask that your universal credit be revised to have the correct amount included from the start of your claim.

- If you were previously getting housing benefit, you should get paid an extra two weeks 'run-on' of housing benefit when you make your universal credit claim to help tide you over until your first universal credit payment.

- Ask for a 'universal credit advance' if you need help while waiting for your first payment.

- You may be able to ask for alternative payment arrangements, so that you have your rent paid directly to your landlord. If you live in Scotland, you may be able to choose to have your rent paid directly to your landlord. Be aware that this may mean that your rent is paid on a different date to when it is due, so it can appear that you are in arrears – talk to your landlord if this happens.

Do you need a loan?

If you need a loan (eg, for a household item you cannot afford or to meet expenses for a new baby or a new job), you can ask for a 'budgeting advance' of universal credit. This is an interest-free loan of universal credit, which you must repay.

You can ask for a budgeting advance for whatever you need, but if you are refused you cannot appeal. To qualify, you must have been on universal credit (or income support, income-based jobseeker's allowance, income-related employment and support allowance or pension credit) for at least six months, unless you need the advance to help you get work or stay in work. Your earnings and any savings or capital resources must also be below a certain level. The maximum you can get depends on your family size. If you have a child, the current maximum (in 2020/21) is £812.

You repay the advance from your universal credit award each month – usually over a 12-month period. You must pay it back in full before you can get another budgeting advance.

EXAMPLE

Budgeting advance

Emma is a lone parent and is getting universal credit. Her washing machine has broken down and she needs a new one. Instead of buying one with expensive high street credit, she asks for a budgeting advance of her universal credit. She pays this back out of her monthly award over the next 12 months.

Can universal credit be paid to other people?

In some circumstances, the Department for Work and Pensions (DWP) can pay part of your universal credit to someone else on your behalf. For example, if you owe money for your fuel or water, the DWP can make deductions from your universal credit award and pay the money directly to the fuel or water company.

If you rent your home, normally the amount for rent in your universal credit is paid to you as part of your monthly award, not to your landlord. It is paid in this way irrespective of whether you rent from a local authority, housing association or private landlord. However, if you are finding it difficult to budget or are building up rent arrears, the DWP may decide to pay your landlord directly under the 'alternative payment arrangements'. This may happen if you or your landlord request this or if the DWP sees that rent arrears are accumulating. Direct payments will always be discussed with you first. If you live in Scotland, you can ask that your rent be paid directly to your landlord – you do not need to have built up arrears.

5. What happens if your circumstances change?

Your circumstances may change while you are getting universal credit. The Department for Work and Pensions (DWP) tells you which changes you should report. You must report all these changes, as well as any other changes that might affect your universal credit award. Phone the universal credit helpline (Monday to Friday 8am to 6pm: 0800 328 5644; textphone 0800 328 1344; Welsh language 0800 328 1744; or if you cannot hear or speak on the phone, Relay UK: 18001 then 0800 328 5644) to report changes. It is best to also report the change on your online journal. You should report the change promptly and always before the end of the monthly 'assessment period' in which the change occurred.

The DWP contacts you online, asking you to confirm the change and telling you whether your award is affected.

If you are employed, you do not usually need to report changes in your earnings – the DWP gets this information from HM Revenue and Customs (HMRC) through its 'real-time information' system. Under this, your employer sends HMRC information about your earnings every time you are paid. However, you may be asked to report your earnings if, for example, your employer is not doing so properly or a report is missing or wrong. If you think the real-time information on your earnings is wrong, send information about what you think is the correct amount to the DWP, even if you have not been asked to report your earnings.

If you are self-employed, you are expected to report your earnings every month on a 'cash in/cash out' basis – ie, the income you have received during the month and payments you have made for that month for any permitted expenses.

If you pay for childcare, you may be asked to report your childcare charges each month.

EXAMPLE

Reporting self-employed earnings

Matt is self-employed. He gets a message from the DWP reminding him to report his earnings for 12 February to 11 March (his monthly assessment period). Matt is busy and does not get round to it. His universal credit award is not paid when it is next due and the DWP tells him that it has been suspended. He must send in the missing earnings report quickly, otherwise his award will stop altogether.

How is your universal credit affected?

You are paid universal credit a month in arrears, so every payment you get is based on your circumstances in the previous month. When you report a change in your circumstances, you must wait until your next universal credit payday before the amount of your award goes up or down. The revised amount is normally worked out as though your new circumstances had lasted for the whole of the previous month. A 'month' means the monthly 'assessment period' on which your payment is based.

If you are late reporting a change (ie, you report it after the end of the assessment period in which the change took place) and the amount of your universal credit increases because of the change, you are not paid arrears before the month you actually reported it, so you will lose money. The Department for Work and Pensions (DWP) can backdate the increase if there are special circumstances, so it is always worth saying why you are reporting a change late and explaining any difficulties you had, such as ill health.

If the amount of your universal credit decreases because of the change, this is backdated to the first day of the monthly assessment period in which the change occurred. So, if you are late reporting the change, you will have been overpaid. The later you report the change, the more the overpayment will be. There is more about overpayments in Chapter 8.

EXAMPLES

Changes in circumstances

Poonam has a new baby on 20 June. This is two weeks into her universal credit assessment period, which ends on 5 July. She tells the DWP on 1 July. Her next payment on 12 July includes an extra £235.83. This is the child element for the whole month in which her baby was born.

Danni has a new baby on 10 July. This is one week into her universal credit assessment period, which ends on 2 August. She is depressed and tired and does not call the DWP until 5 August. She is paid her usual amount on 9 August, with no extra amount for her baby. She is paid an extra £235.83 for the baby on 9 September. She has lost a month's extra money. If Danni had explained why she was late reporting the birth, the DWP could have decided to pay the additional amount from 9 August.

Steve starts university on 6 October. This is three weeks into his universal credit assessment period, which ends on 14 October. He tells the DWP on 6 October. He is no longer entitled to universal credit as a student and so his award stops. On his next payday on 21 October, he gets no universal credit.

Further information

The DWP has produced a basic guide *Universal Credit and You*, available at gov.uk/government/publications/universal-credit-and-you. There is more detailed guidance available at gov.uk/government/collections/universal-credit-information-for-stakeholders-and-partners.

You can find details on your local authority's local welfare assistance scheme via advicelocal.uk.

More information about universal credit claims and payments is in CPAG's *Welfare Benefits and Tax Credits Handbook*.

Chapter 5
The amount of universal credit

This chapter covers:

1. What is the maximum amount of universal credit?

2. How do your income and capital affect universal credit?

3. How much universal credit do you get?

What you need to know

- Universal credit includes an amount for you and your partner. This is called the 'standard allowance'.

- Amounts for children for whom you are responsible are added to the standard allowance. These are called 'child elements'. There is an additional amount if your child is disabled.

- Extra amounts are added to the standard allowance, depending on your circumstances. You may get an additional amount if you or your partner are ill or disabled, or if you or your partner are caring for a disabled person. There are also amounts to help with your rent (and some other housing costs), and for childcare costs. When the official transfer process starts, you may get an additional amount included (a 'transitional element') to ensure you are not worse off when you are transferred to universal credit from your old benefits or tax credits. But that does not apply if you transfer outside the official process.

- If you have other income, this reduces the amount of universal credit to which you are entitled, although some income is ignored.

- You are not entitled to universal credit if you and your partner have more than £16,000 capital.

1. What is the maximum amount of universal credit?

Universal credit is a 'means-tested benefit'. This means that the amount you get depends on your family circumstances and on how much other income (if any) you have. As your income increases, the amount of your universal credit award reduces.

Your 'maximum universal credit' is made up of a 'standard allowance' and amounts (called 'elements') for:

- each child (limited to two children in some circumstances)
- each disabled child (at a lower or higher rate)
- you or your partner if you are ill or disabled
- you or your partner if you care for a disabled person
- your rent and certain other housing costs
- your childcare costs

When the official 'managed migration' process starts, you may also have a 'transitional element' included to ensure you are not worse off when you are transferred to universal credit from your old benefits or tax credits.

Each of these amounts has its own qualifying conditions. The rest of this section explains when these amounts apply and how your maximum amount of universal credit is worked out. If you have no income or your income is below a certain level, you get the maximum amount of universal credit. However, this may be reduced by the government's 'benefit cap'.

The standard allowance

Universal credit includes an amount for you and your partner, if you have one. This is called the 'standard allowance'. How much you get depends on your age and whether you are claiming as a single person or jointly with your partner.

Note: these amounts were subject to special increases for 2020/21, in the light of the coronavirus pandemic. It is not clear whether these increases will also apply in 2021/22.

Monthly rates of standard allowance, 2020/21	
Single claimant, under 25	£342.72
Single claimant, 25 or over	£409.89
Joint claimants, both under 25	£488.59
Joint claimants, at least one 25 or over	£594.04

Child element

If you are responsible for any children, your universal credit includes an additional amount (called a 'child element') for each child under 16. You can also get a child element for each 'qualifying young person' who is aged 16 to 18 (or 19 in some cases) and who is, for example, still at school or college on a non-advanced course.

Note: you get a child element for all children born before 6 April 2017. You cannot usually get a child element for a third or subsequent child born on or after 6 April 2017, but there are exceptions. There is more information about this 'two-child limit' in Chapter 10.

Monthly rates of child element, 2020/21	
First child/qualifying young person if born before 6 April 2017	£281.25
Each other child/qualifying young person	£235.83

If your first or only child was born before 6 April 2017, the child element is £281.25. For any other child the amount is £235.83. For example, if you have two children, both born after 6 April 2017, you get a child element of £235.83 for each child.

A child can only be included in one universal credit claim. So if your child normally lives with more than one person (eg, if you are separated from your partner and your child lives with both of you), whoever has the main responsibility for the child can claim universal credit for her/him.

You cannot normally be responsible for a child if s/he is being 'looked after' by the local authority. The exceptions to this are if the child is living with you and you have parental responsibility for her/him, or if s/he is being is looked after because s/he is away for a planned short respite break.

Additional amount if your child is disabled

If your child is disabled, your universal credit includes an additional amount. There are two levels of payment, depending on the severity of your child's disability.

- You get the lower amount if your child gets disability living allowance or personal independence payment.

- You get the higher amount if your child gets the highest rate of disability living allowance 'care component', the enhanced rate of personal independence payment 'daily living component', or if s/he is certified as severely sight impaired or blind.

Monthly additional amounts for a disabled child, 2020/21	
Lower amount	£128.25
Higher amount	£400.29

Even if you do not get a 'child element' for your child because of the 'two-child limit', you still get the additional amount if s/he is disabled.

Additional amount if you or your partner are ill or disabled

If you or your partner are ill or disabled, you may be able to get an additional amount added to your 'standard allowance'. You do not get this automatically. For example, you may get personal independence payment because of your disability, but this, in itself, does not mean you get an additional amount in your universal credit. To get the additional amount, you must be assessed as having 'limited capability for work-related activity'. Before 3 April 2017, a lower additional amount was added to your standard allowance if you were assessed as having 'limited capability for work'. In general, if your period of limited capability for work started on or after 3 April 2017, the 'limited capability for work element' is not included.

Monthly additional amounts for ill health or disability, 2020/21	
Limited capability for work element (only if your limited capability for work started before 3 April 2017)	£128.25
Limited capability for work-related activity element	£341.92

Note: although there is no additional amount for limited capability for work in new claims from 3 April 2017, it can still be important to be assessed as having limited capability for work. This is because you can then keep a certain amount of your earnings before your universal credit is affected (called a 'work allowance') and you have fewer 'work-related requirements'.

In some circumstances, you are treated as having limited capability for work without having to be assessed. For example, this applies if you are a hospital patient (this can be extended from when you leave hospital until you have recovered), or if you are in residential rehabilitation for drug or alcohol problems.

In some circumstances, you can also be treated as having limited capability for work-related activity without having to be assessed. For example, this applies if you are terminally ill or you are having chemotherapy or radiotherapy for cancer (or are likely to do so in the next six months), or if you are recovering from this treatment. If you have already been assessed as having limited capability for work-related activity for employment and support allowance, you are treated as having limited capability for work-related activity for universal credit and should get the element straight away.

Box A

The work capability assessment

'Limited capability for work' is a test of whether your health problems or disabilities mean that you are currently unable to work. The assessment usually involves your completing a questionnaire and attending a medical examination. To pass the test, you must score 15 points on a list of specified activities. You are likely to be assessed regularly to check whether you still meet these conditions. If you do not complete the questionnaire about your health problems or do not attend the medical without a good reason, you are likely to be treated as not satisfying the conditions.

You are also assessed to decide whether you have '**limited capability for work-related activity**'. This test identifies whether your illness or disability is so serious that you should not be expected to think about returning to work at the moment. To pass the test, you must meet one of a list of specified activities (called 'descriptors').

You may be regularly assessed to check whether you still meet these conditions.

The work capability assessment is also used to decide whether you qualify for employment and support allowance. If you get employment and support allowance, you do not need to have a separate assessment for universal credit.

Usually, you do not get an additional element in your universal credit straight away. There is usually a 'waiting period' of at least three months. If you are are terminally ill, and in some other circumstances, there is no waiting period.

If both you and your partner have limited capability for work and/or limited capability for work-related activity, you only get one element. You get the higher element that applies. You cannot get the limited capability for work element or the limited capability for work-related activity element in addition to the 'carer element'. You get the highest one that applies. However, if you are in a couple, one of you can qualify for the limited capability for work/limited capability for work-related activity element and the other can qualify for the carer element.

If you are getting either the limited capability for work or limited capability for work-related activity element and you start work, you do not automatically lose the element, but your capability may be reassessed. **Note:** if you are not getting one of these elements and are already in work and your weekly earnings are at least 16 times the national minimum wage, you can only be assessed for these elements if you get disability living allowance, personal independence payment or attendance allowance.

Coronavirus

During the coronavirus pandemic, the Department for Work and Pensions (DWP) suspended face-to-face medical assessments. Instead, assessments can be carried out by other means – eg, via a telephone interview. However, in practice some claimants reported long delays in being assessed. There are no rules on how quickly an assessment must be carried out, so if you are having to wait a long time, contact the DWP to ask what the reason is and complain if you remain unhappy.

Additional amount if you or your partner are a carer

If you are caring for someone who is severely disabled, you may get an additional amount added to your 'standard allowance'. This is called the 'carer element'.

Monthly rate of carer element, 2020/21	
Carer element	£162.92

You can get the carer element if you are caring for a severely disabled person for at least 35 hours a week. The person you care for must get attendance allowance, the middle or highest rate of disability living allowance 'care component', or either rate of the personal independence payment 'daily living component'. The easiest way to qualify is to claim carer's allowance, which is a benefit for carers. However, even if you do not get carer's allowance, you can still get the carer element if you care for the person for at least 35 hours a week. This is the case even if your earnings are too high to claim carer's allowance. Only one person can get the carer element for a disabled person, even if more than one person is caring for her/him.

Coronavirus

During the coronavirus pandemic, special rules mean that you can have a temporary break in caring if you have COVID-19 or are isolating because of coronavirus symptoms. These rules were due to cease to apply on 30 November 2020.

If both you and your partner satisfy the rules for the carer element, you get two elements, but not if you are both caring for the same disabled person.

You cannot get the 'limited capability for work element' or the 'limited capability for work-related activity element' in addition to the carer element. You get the highest one that applies. However, if you are in a couple, one of you can qualify for the carer element and the other can qualify for the limited capability for work or limited capability for work-related activity element.

EXAMPLE

One member of a couple is ill, the other is a carer

Jim has cancer and is recovering from chemotherapy. Barbara is looking after him. Jim gets personal independence payment daily living component. Their universal credit includes a limited capability for work-related activity element of £341.92 and a carer element of £162.92 a month.

Housing costs element

Universal credit can include an amount for certain housing costs. This is called the 'housing costs element'. The housing costs element can cover your rent and some service charges. It usually only covers the housing costs for the home you live in. However, in certain situations, it can be paid for a home you are not living in. For example, if you are prevented from moving into a new home because you are waiting for disability adaptations to be carried out, the housing costs element can be included for up to one month before you move in.

There are also limited situations in which you can receive a housing costs element for two homes. For example, if you are disabled and you are waiting for a new home to be adapted, it can be paid for two homes for up to one month. If you are fleeing domestic violence and are living in temporary accommodation but intend to return home, the housing costs element can be paid on both homes for up to 12 months.

Sometimes, you cannot get a housing costs element – eg, if you are paying rent to a close relative and you are also living with her/him.

If you have a mortgage, you may be able to get a loan from the Department for Work and Pensions to help you pay the interest.

Note: the rules on housing costs may be different in Scotland at some point in the future.

Help with your rent

The amount included in your universal credit to help you with your rent depends on how many people are in your family and on your circumstances.

If you are renting from a local authority or housing association, the amount of the 'housing costs element' is based on the rent you pay, plus certain service charges. However, the amount may be reduced if you are considered to be living in a property that is too big for you. This is often called the 'bedroom tax'. See Box B for how many bedrooms you are allowed.

Box B
How many bedrooms are you allowed?

You are allowed one bedroom for each of the following:

- a couple
- someone aged 16 or over
- two children of the same gender
- two children aged under 10
- any other child
- a carer (or carers) providing overnight care to a disabled child or adult

In some circumstances, you may be allowed an additional bedroom – eg, if you have a child with a disability or if you are a couple but cannot share a room with your partner because of a disability.

If you have one more bedroom than you are allowed, your housing costs element is reduced by 14 per cent of your rent. If you have two or more additional bedrooms, your housing costs element is reduced by 25 per cent of your rent.

EXAMPLE

Housing costs element

Tess is a lone parent with two children – a boy aged 10 and a girl aged 12. She is allowed three bedrooms under the universal credit rules. Her housing association house has four bedrooms and her monthly rent is £400. Her housing costs element is reduced by 14 per cent of her rent (£56). Her housing costs element is £344 (£400 – £56).

If you are renting from a private landlord, the amount of the housing costs element is limited to the 'local housing allowance' in your area for the size of property you are assessed as needing.

The number of bedrooms you are allowed is the same as in Box B, except that there is a maximum of four.

If you are single, aged under 35 and have no dependants, you are usually only eligible for a housing costs element to cover the rent for a room in shared accommodation.

The amount of the housing costs element you get to help with your rent (whether you rent from a local authority, housing association or private landlord) is reduced if you have any 'non-dependants' living with you. A 'non-dependant' is someone, such as an adult daughter or son or another relative, who shares your home. A set amount of £75.15 a month (in 2020/21) for each non-dependant is deducted from the housing costs element, even if you do not receive any contribution from that person towards your rent. However, there are some situations in which no amount is deducted – eg, if you or the non-dependant are getting the middle or highest rate of the disability living allowance 'care component' or the personal independence payment 'daily living component', or if your non-dependant is under 21 years old.

What CPAG says

Deductions for non-dependants

If you have a non-dependant living with you, check that your housing costs element has been worked out correctly, as sometimes a deduction is made when it should not be.

If the amount of your universal credit does not cover the full cost of your rent, you may be able to get a 'discretionary housing payment' from your local authority to make up the difference.

Note: if you live in certain types of 'specified accommodation' (including where you get care, support or supervision) or temporary homeless accommodation, your universal credit does not include a housing costs element – you can get housing benefit to help with your rent instead. Chapter 2 explains who is affected by this.

Help with service charges if you are an owner-occupier

If you own your home, you may get a 'housing costs element' in your universal credit to help with certain service charges. However, you do not get an amount included if you are doing any paid work, irrespective of how few hours you work.

You do not usually get any help with your service charges during the first nine months of your universal credit claim. You may be able to get help earlier if you were previously getting income support, jobseeker's allowance or employment and support allowance.

If the housing costs element stops being included in your universal credit award (eg, because you have started work), you must wait nine months after stopping work before it can be included again.

Childcare costs element

Your universal credit can include an amount for your childcare costs (the 'childcare costs element') if you are in paid work (or are about to start paid work) and you are paying for formal childcare, such as a registered childminder, nursery or after-school club. Childcare costs can be paid for a child up to 1 September following her/his 16th birthday.

You must be:

- a lone parent
- a couple and both of you are working
- a couple and one of you is working and the other has 'limited capability for work', or is caring for a disabled person or is temporarily away from home

You are treated as working if you are getting statutory sick pay, maternity allowance or statutory maternity, adoption, paternity or shared parental pay.

You can get this element irrespective of how few hours you work. However, the childcare costs must be necessary to enable you to take up, or continue in, paid work or to enable you to maintain your childcare arrangements allowing you to return to work – eg, after maternity leave.

The childcare costs element in 2020/21 is 85 per cent of your actual childcare costs, up to a maximum of £646.35 a month for one child or £1,108.04 for two or more children.

Coronavirus

The Department for Work and Pensions has confirmed that the childcare costs element can only cover costs for childcare that has actually taken place, including during the coronavirus pandemic. So, for example, the element will not apply to a 'retainer' or similar fee paid to a childcare provider.

EXAMPLES

Childcare costs element

Amara is a lone parent with one child. She is working and has childcare costs of £600 a month. Amara gets a childcare costs element of £510 a month in her maximum universal credit amount – ie, 85 per cent of £600.

Ffion and Darren have two children and both work. Their childcare costs are £1,200 a month. They get a childcare costs element of £1,020 a month in their maximum universal credit amount – ie, 85 per cent of £1,200.

What CPAG says

Advance childcare costs

Some childcare providers require a deposit or advance payment of fees before they will confirm a childcare place. However, you may not be able to start work until the childcare place is available and cannot afford to pay for the childcare until you have received your first wages. Even if a childcare provider is prepared to wait for payment, the childcare costs element in universal credit can only be included after you have actually paid the provider. If you need help to pay for childcare before you start work, or before the end of your assessment period, request a 'budgeting advance' of universal credit. However, these payments are discretionary and must be repaid within 12 months. You cannot get a budgeting advance again if you are still repaying an earlier one.

If a budgeting advance is refused, or the amount is not enough, ask your 'work coach' about getting help through the Flexible Support Fund. This is available to Jobcentre Plus staff, and payments are not repayable. However, if some of your childcare costs are covered by a payment from the Flexible Support Fund or other support, the same amount cannot also be covered by universal credit.

Providing evidence

You must report your childcare costs by the end of the assessment period that follows the assessment period in which you paid them (if later, give your reasons for the delay) and you can be asked to provide further information or evidence, usually within 14 days. If you have been asked for proof of your payments, but your childcare provider does not give monthly receipts and so your childcare costs are not included in your universal credit because you were unable to provide evidence in time, ask for a 'mandatory reconsideration' of the decision and appeal if necessary.

You may be given conflicting information about whether to upload evidence to your online journal, hand it in to the job centre or post it. Any of these methods should be acceptable.

EXAMPLES

Maximum universal credit

Michael and Sharmani are a couple aged 45 and 46 with two children under 10 (born before 6 April 2017). None of the family have health problems. The couple live in a two-bedroom local authority flat with a monthly rent of £300. They have no childcare costs.

Standard allowance £594.04

Child element x two £517.08

Housing costs element £300

Maximum universal credit = £1,411.12

Marcia is a lone parent aged 30 with one child (born before 6 April 2017). She lives in a three-bedroom housing association house and her rent is £350 a month. The house has one more bedroom than Marcia is allowed, so her housing costs element is reduced by 14 per cent of the rent. Marcia's child has a disability and gets the lowest rate of disability living allowance care component. She pays £200 a month for childcare.

Standard allowance £409.89

Child element £281.25

Amount for disabled child £128.25

Housing costs element £301

Childcare costs element £170

Maximum universal credit = £1,290.39

Note: in both examples, if the eldest child was born on or after 6 April 2017, the amount of the child element for that child would be reduced.

2. How do your income and capital affect universal credit?

If you and your partner have any income or capital, your universal credit may be affected. Your income could be your earnings or other income, such as other benefits. Your capital includes savings and some property. As your income increases, the amount of universal credit you get usually decreases.

Income and capital belonging to your children is ignored.

How do your earnings affect universal credit?

Your net earnings from employment or self-employment may affect the amount of universal credit you get.

'Net earnings' means your earnings after deducting tax, national insurance and any contribution to an occupational pension scheme.

Statutory sick pay and statutory maternity, paternity, shared parental and adoption pay also count as earnings.

Your 'maximum universal credit' is reduced by a proportion of your earnings. This is often called the 'taper' – ie, the rate at which your universal credit tapers away as your earnings increase. The taper is 63 per cent. This means that your universal credit is reduced by 63 pence for every pound you earn.

Some people can earn a certain amount (known as a 'work allowance') before their universal credit is affected.

If you have a child, or if you or your partner have 'limited capability for work', a work allowance is deducted from your earnings before your universal credit starts being reduced. The amount of the work allowance depends on whether you have a 'housing costs element' included in your universal credit. A household can only have one work allowance, even if you are a couple and both of you have earnings.

Amount of monthly work allowance, 2020/21	
Universal credit includes a housing costs element	£292
Universal credit does not include a housing costs element	£512

EXAMPLES

Work allowance

Jon and Barry are a couple with two children. They have a housing costs element included in their universal credit award. Their work allowance is £292 a month.

Ruby is single and has no children. She has limited capability for work. She has no housing costs element included in her universal credit award. Her work allowance is £512 a month.

Florence is a lone parent with one child. She owns her own home and pays a service charge, but because she is working there is no housing costs element included in her universal credit award. Her work allowance is £512 a month.

Note: if your universal credit stops because your earnings are too high and you reclaim universal credit within six months, you may be treated as still having some of that income.

How are your earnings assessed?

Your employer is required to report your earnings to HM Revenue and Customs every month. This is called 'real-time information'. If your earnings are reported by your employer in this way, the figure used in the universal credit assessment is taken from the amount in the reports received by the Department for Work and Pensions (DWP). If your employer does not report your earnings in time, the DWP may ask you to give this information instead.

The earnings figure used in the universal credit calculation is the amount you received in each universal credit 'assessment period', which is one calendar month. This means that your monthly amount of universal credit will change if your earnings go up or down.

EXAMPLE

Earnings figure

Bert's first universal credit assessment period starts on 8 July 2020. Each assessment period after that starts on the 8th of the month. In the first assessment period (from 8 July to 7 August) he has earnings which are paid on 25 July. This is the earnings figure used to calculate his universal credit for the period 8 July to 7 August.

What CPAG says

Monthly payments

The frequency of when you are paid your wages or salary may not correspond with your universal credit assessment periods. For example, you may be paid every four weeks, not every calendar month. This, or some other reason, might result in your having two paydays in one monthly assessment period. If that happens, it is likely that the DWP will calculate your universal credit for that one assessment period as if you have a much higher income than usual. In legal challenges, the courts have ruled that this is not lawful in all cases, but left it to the government to resolve. If you feel that you have been disadvantaged by having two paydays count in one assessment period, see the information about test cases on CPAG's website (cpag.org.uk/welfare-rights/legal-test-cases) and seek advice.

If you get no payment in a particular month, your universal credit will not restart automatically the following month. You must log in to your account to restart your claim. This should just mean confirming your details are the same as before.

Are you self-employed?

If you are self-employed, you must report your income and expenses to the DWP every month. There is a special online tool for this. Expenses can include regular costs like rent or wages, purchase of stock and utility bills. Flat-rate deductions are made for some expenses, such as mileage. If you make a loss, this can be carried forward and deducted from any profit made in subsequent months.

If you are self-employed and on a low income, you may be assumed to have a higher income than you actually have. After 12 months of being on universal credit while self-employed, you may be treated as earning at least the national minimum wage for someone of your age for the number of hours the DWP expects you to search for work. This is called the 'minimum income floor'. However, if you are not working regularly (eg, because there is little work available or you are unwell), that may indicate you are not in 'gainful self-employment' and you should not be treated as having income that you do not have.

Coronavirus

During the coronavirus pandemic, the government has temporarily suspended applying the minimum income floor. This suspension was due to apply until 12 November 2020. This means that during this period you will not be assumed to have a higher income that you actually have.

Do you have other income?

Only certain types of other income are taken into account for universal credit. For example, the following counts:

- occupational and personal pensions
- certain benefits, including contribution-based jobseeker's allowance and contributory employment and support allowance
- maintenance for you or your spouse or partner, but not child maintenance
- student loans and some grants
- certain insurance payments
- income from an annuity or certain trusts

Disability living allowance, personal independence payment, attendance allowance, bereavement support payment, war pensions and child benefit are not taken into account as income, nor is income from lodgers.

Income (other than earnings) that is taken into account reduces your maximum universal credit pound for pound.

Do you have any capital?

Any capital you have may affect your universal credit. 'Capital' includes savings, stocks and shares, property and trusts. Certain types of capital are ignored – eg, property that is your main home, personal injury payments placed in a trust fund, some other compensation payments and, for at least six months, your former home that you are trying to sell. Any capital owned by your children is ignored.

If you and your partner have capital of more than £16,000 (in 2020/ 21), you cannot get universal credit. The one exception to this is if you move from tax credits to universal credit as part of the 'managed migration' process – any capital you have over £16,000 is ignored for one year.

You are treated as still having capital if you deliberately get rid of it in order to get universal credit or to increase the amount of universal credit you get. This does not apply if you have used the capital to reduce or pay a debt, or to pay for goods or services which are considered reasonable.

Is your capital more than £6,000?

If your capital is more than £6,000 but £16,000 or less, you are treated as having an income of £4.35 a month for every £250 (or part of £250) over £6,000, regardless of whether you actually receive this income – eg, in the form of interest on your savings.

EXAMPLE

Income from capital

Niamh has £7,400 savings. This is £1,400 more than £6,000. She is treated as having an income from this capital of £26.10 a month (£4.35 for every £250, or part of £250, over £6,000). This income reduces her maximum universal credit pound for pound.

3. How much universal credit do you get?

How do you calculate universal credit?

Follow the steps below to work out your entitlement. Universal credit is worked out on a month-by-month basis.

Step one: calculate your maximum universal credit
Add together your 'standard allowance', any additional amounts because you have children, any additional amounts for special circumstances (such as the 'carer element') and any 'housing costs element'. You may also have a 'transitional element'. The total is your 'maximum universal credit'.

If you have no other income, this total is the amount of universal credit you get. However, if you are subject to the 'benefit cap', the amount you get may be restricted. If you have other income, go to Step two.

Step two: work out your income, other than earnings
Your income might include other benefits (such as contributory employment and support allowance), an occupational pension or income from capital. Remember that some benefits, including disability living allowance, personal independence payment and child benefit, are ignored. Your income is worked out on a monthly basis.

Step three: work out your earnings and how much can be ignored
Work out your net earnings received for the month after tax, national insurance and any contribution you make to an occupational pension have been deducted. If you are an employee, this is usually the

amount reported by your employer through the 'real-time information' system, so it is likely to be the same as the information on your payslip. If you are self-employed, you may be treated as having higher earnings than you actually have.

Check whether a 'work allowance' applies to you and, if so, deduct it from your net earnings. Calculate 63 per cent of the resulting figure.

Step four: calculate your total income
Combine the income to be taken into account in Steps two and three.

Step five: calculate your universal credit entitlement
Deduct your total income to be taken into account (Step four) from your maximum universal credit (Step one). This is the amount of universal credit you get. However, the amount you get may be restricted by the 'benefit cap'.

EXAMPLE

Lone parent with two children

Sophia is aged 30. She lives in a housing association rented property and is not affected by the 'bedroom tax'. Her rent is £480 a month. She does not have any health problems and she is not looking after a severely disabled person. Her two children, who were both born after 6 April 2017, do not have any disabilities. She has no other income apart from child benefit. Her monthly universal credit is calculated as follows.

Step one: calculate your maximum universal credit
Standard allowance £409.89

Child element x two £471.66

Housing costs element £480

Total = £1,361.55

Sophia has no income apart from child benefit, which is disregarded. She therefore gets her maximum amount of universal credit (£1,361.55). She does not need to follow the remaining steps.

EXAMPLE

Couple with one child

Rob and Gwen are aged 31 and 32. They live in a two-bedroom local authority flat. Their rent is £300 a month. Their child, who was born before 6 April 2017, has a disability and receives the lowest rate care component of disability living allowance. Their only other income is child benefit and contributory employment and support allowance of £322.18 a month, which Rob has been getting since March 2020 because he has limited capability for work. Their monthly universal credit is calculated as follows.

Step one: calculate your maximum universal credit
Standard allowance £594.04

Child element £281.25

Disabled child addition £128.25

Housing costs element £300

Total = £1,303.54

Step two: work out your income, other than earnings
Employment and support allowance £322.18 (disability living allowance and child benefit are disregarded).

Step three: work out your earnings and how much can be ignored
Rob and Gwen do not have any earnings.

Step four: calculate your total income
Their total income is £322.18.

Step five: calculate your universal credit entitlement
£1,303.54 − £322.18 = £981.36

EXAMPLE

Single person

Imran is aged 24. He is single and has no children. He has a disability and receives the standard rate of the daily living component and the enhanced rate of the mobility component of personal independence payment. He has limited capability for work, which began after 3 April 2017. He lives in a housing association flat and is not affected by the 'bedroom tax'. His rent is £400 a month. Imran has net earnings of £416 a month. His monthly universal credit is calculated as follows.

Step one: calculate your maximum universal credit
Standard allowance £342.72

Housing costs element £400

Total = £742.72

Step two: work out your income, other than earnings
Personal independence payment is disregarded and, therefore, Imran has no income other than his earnings.

Step three: work out your earnings and how much can be ignored
Imran has £416 a month net earnings.

The work allowance that applies to Imran is £292.

£416 – £292 = £124

£124 x 63% = £78.12

Step four: calculate your total income
Imran's total income is £78.12.

Step five: calculate your universal credit entitlement
£742.72 – £78.12 = £664.60

EXAMPLE

Couple with one child

Carl and Meg are a couple aged 30 and 29, with one child who was born on 5 May 2018. Meg works and earns £700 net a month. Carl gets £492.05 a month contributory employment and support allowance because he has limited capability for work-related activity. Their only other income is child benefit. They live in a housing association house. The rent is £450 a month. The 'bedroom tax' does not apply. They have no childcare costs. Their universal credit is calculated as follows.

Step one: calculate your maximum universal credit
Standard allowance £594.04

Child element £235.83

Limited capability for work-related activity element £341.92

Housing costs element £450

Total = £1,621.79

Step two: work out your income, other than earnings
Carl's employment and support allowance of £492.052 counts in full as income.

Step three: work out your earnings and how much can be ignored
Meg has £700 a month net earnings.

The work allowance that applies to Meg and Carl is £292.

£700 − £292 = £408

£408 x 63% = £257.04

Step four: calculate your total income
£492.05 contributory employment and support allowance plus £257.04 earnings = £749.09

Step five: calculate your universal credit entitlement
£1,621.79 − £749.09 = £872.70

Have you been transferred to universal credit?

If you are getting an old 'means-tested benefit' or tax credit, at some point in the future, the Department for Work and Pensions (DWP) will transfer your claim to universal credit. The DWP calls this official process 'managed migration'. There is more information about the transfer process in Chapter 2. **Note:** at the time of writing, the rules on managed migration had not been finalised and may therefore change. The DWP had started to test the managed migration process but that testing was suspended during the coronavirus pandemic. At time of writing, it was not clear when the process would recommence.

When the process begins, if you are transferred to universal credit as part of managed migration, your universal credit may include an additional amount, called a 'transitional element'. That is intended to ensure that the amount you get when you move on to universal credit is not less than the amount you were getting on your previous benefit(s).

The transitional element is calculated by comparing the total amount of all your old benefits and tax credits on the day before you became entitled to universal credit (the DWP calls this the 'total legacy amount') with the amount of universal credit you would have been entitled to on the same day (the DWP calls this the 'indicative universal credit amount').

If the 'total legacy amount' is more than than 'indicative universal credit' amount, you get a transitional element to make up the difference. This is added to your maximum universal credit. The amount will reduce over time as the other amounts in your maximum universal credit, apart from the childcare costs element, increase.

If you have certain changes in your circumstances, the transitional element stops – eg, if you stop claiming as a single person and start claiming as a couple. If your universal credit entitlement stops for more than three months, the element will not be included if you then claim again.

You will only get a transitional element if you are transferred to universal credit by the DWP as part of the managed migration process, not if you make a claim for universal credit yourself – eg, after a change of circumstances.

When you transfer to universal credit having made a claim yourself rather than under the managed migration process, that is called 'natural migration'. Because you do not get a transitional element under natural migration, you may be worse off under universal credit than under your old benefits, although this depends on the facts in your case.

Box C
Severely disabled people

If you are entitled to a 'severe disability premium' in your old benefit, until 27 January 2021 you are prevented from claiming universal credit and so cannot transfer to it under 'natural migration'. However, if you transferred to universal credit by natural migration before 16 January 2019 when this rule was introduced, you may be entitled to an extra amount of universal credit. The DWP calls this a 'transitional SDP amount'. You may also get a transitional SDP amount in other circumstances – eg, if you have correctly been allowed to claim universal credit and so transfer to it but get a backdated award of the severe disability premium, which had it been in payment at the time you would have been prevented from claiming universal credit. If you are wrongly allowed to claim universal credit before 27 January 2021 (ie, you are entitled to the severe disability premium but the DWP mistakenly allow you to claim universal credit), the DWP may put you back on to your old benefit if you request that.

A severe disability premium was included in your (or your partner's) means-tested benefit if at the time of your claim for universal credit you (or your partner) were getting a qualifying disability benefit (such as the 'daily living component' of personal independence payment), no one got carer's allowance for looking after you, and you technically counted as living alone. If that applies you will be entitled to a transitional SDP amount, backdated to the start of your universal credit award. If you receive arrears as a lump sum, this is ignored as your capital for up to 12 months.

Monthly rates of transitional SDP 2020/21

Single people

Not getting limited capability for work-related activity element	£285
Getting limited capability for work-related activity element	£120
Couples who previously got the lower rate of the severe disability premium	
Not getting limited capability for work-related activity element	£285
Getting limited capability for work-related activity element	£120
Couples who previously got the higher rate of the severe disability premium	£405

Will the amount of your universal credit be restricted?

Your monthly benefit entitlement may be restricted to a level set by the government. This is known as the 'benefit cap'.

Benefit cap, 2020/21

	London	Outside London
Single person, no dependent children	£1,284.17	£1,116.67
Everyone else	£1,916.67	£1,666.67

Your 'benefit entitlement' includes universal credit and most other benefits, but does not include pension credit or retirement pension. If your benefit entitlement is more than the cap level, the excess is deducted from your universal credit. If you have a 'childcare costs element' included in your universal credit, this amount is deducted from the excess before your universal credit is reduced. If the childcare costs element is more than the excess, no deduction is made.

Are you exempt from the benefit cap?

You may be exempt from the 'benefit cap' in certain circumstances.

- You are getting personal independence payment, disability living allowance, attendance allowance or industrial injuries disablement benefit.
- You are getting carer's allowance or the 'carer element' in your universal credit.
- You are getting guardian's allowance.
- Your child gets disability living allowance or personal independence payment.
- You have 'limited capability for work-related activity'.
- You are a war pensioner, or a war widow/widower.
- You earn an amount equal to working 16 hours a week at the 'national living wage' converted to a net monthly amount (called the 'earnings exception threshold').

If you have been working for at least a year earning at least the amount of the earnings exception threshold and you stop working, you are exempt from the benefit cap for nine months.

Further information

You can check the local housing allowance that applies to you at lha-direct.voa.gov.uk/search.aspx.
There is more information about universal credit amounts, and how income and capital is worked out, in CPAG's *Welfare Benefits and Tax Credits Handbook*.

Chapter 6
Your responsibilities

This chapter covers:

1. What is the claimant commitment?

2. What are you expected to do?

3. Who must look for work?

4. Who must prepare for work?

5. Who must take part in work-focused interviews?

6. Who has no work-related requirements?

What you need to know

- To get universal credit, you must accept a 'claimant commitment'.

- If you claim jointly as a couple with your partner, s/he must also accept a claimant commitment.

- If you or your partner do not accept your claimant commitments, you are not entitled to universal credit, either as a couple or as a single person.

- Your claimant commitment lists your general responsibilities while getting universal credit. These 'work-related requirements' range from being immediately available for and searching for full-time work to having no requirements at all.

- You can be told to take specific actions by other methods such as a message in your universal credit online journal or by text.

- If you already work but your earnings are low, you may be expected to look for more work or better paid work.

1. What is the claimant commitment?

When you claim universal credit, you must usually accept a 'claimant commitment' before you can get any benefit. Your claimant commitment is an agreement between you and the Department for Work and Pensions (DWP). It is a record of your general responsibilities, including the 'work-related requirements' you must meet, while you are receiving universal credit. These are usually set after an interview with your DWP 'work coach'.

If you are making a joint claim with your partner, s/he must also accept her/his own claimant commitment, otherwise neither of you will get any universal credit. If you are part of a couple but you are awarded universal credit as a single person, because your partner, for example, is a 'person subject to immigration control', your partner does not need to accept a claimant commitment because s/he is not a claimant.

Your claimant commitment can be changed or updated if your circumstances change. If it is changed, you must accept the new version to continue getting universal credit.

If you do not agree with the work-related requirements in your claimant commitment, you can ask the DWP to review it. However, while it is being reviewed, you must accept the claimant commitment in order to get paid universal credit. You should also keep to your work-related requirements, otherwise you may be given a 'sanction' and the amount of your universal credit may be reduced.

What does a claimant commitment include?

The 'claimant commitment' sets out what you must generally do in return for receiving universal credit. This includes what 'work-related requirements' are expected of you.

Your initial claimant commitment is usually drawn up by your 'work coach' in a meeting after you claim. It includes the following information.

- Your general work-related requirements.

- Details of specific things you must do, and by when.

- If you must look for work, the kind of work you are looking for, the number of hours you are expected to spend searching for work and when you are expected to be available for work.

- By how much your universal credit will be reduced, and for how long, if you do not meet your requirements and your award is sanctioned (see Chapter 7).

- Details of your right to challenge a decision to sanction your universal credit. Chapter 9 has more information on challenging decisions you do not agree with.

- An instruction to report changes in your circumstances, and what happens if you do not do so.

You can also be required to take specific actions, such as applying for a particular job or attending a course, that are part of meeting your general work-related requirements. Your claimant commitment does not need to be updated each time you are given one of these specific actions. You should always be given any specific actions in a

---

EXAMPLE

The claimant commitment

Jenny is 32 and lives alone. She loses her job and claims universal credit. Her claimant commitment says that she must look for work and will do anything she can to get work. It states that she must be available for suitable work at any time. There is a section about the type of work that she is looking for initially, and what she must do every week to look for work. This includes that she must normally spend 35 hours a week searching for work, regular things she must do every week, and specific actions to be taken by the end of the month. It explains the sanctions that may apply if she does not meet these requirements and her right to challenge any decision to reduce the amount of her universal credit. It states that she must report any relevant changes of circumstances, and the possible consequences if she does not do so.

written form, such as a note in your online universal credit journal or an appointment card, so that these instructions can be referred back to if there is any dispute about whether you did the specific actions. However you are told to take these specific actions, you should always be given adequate notice as well as detailed instructions of exactly what you have to do, where you have to go and at what time, and the consequences of not doing the specific action. If you do not understand anything about a specific action you have been given, you should contact your work coach immediately.

How do you accept a claimant commitment?

The Department for Work and Pensions (DWP) decides how you must accept your 'claimant commitment'. You can be asked to accept it online, by telephone or in person. Usually, the DWP asks you to make an appointment at your local job centre to discuss and accept your claimant commitment once you have completed your online claim.

If you do not accept your claimant commitment within the time allowed by the DWP, you are not entitled and you do not get universal credit, unless the DWP agrees to extend the time limit.

Coronavirus

During the coronavirus pandemic, you might not be required to attend face-to-face appointments at job centres. Instead, if you make a new claim for universal credit, the DWP may phone you to gather any further information it needs and agree your claimant commitment. Any further contact might then be online or by phone until the DWP decides it is safe to have a face-to-face appointment at a job centre. As the lockdown is eased, the DWP is reviewing its policies and has said that all existing claimant commitments will be reviewed.

What happens if you do not accept a claimant commitment?

If you do not accept a 'claimant commitment', you are not entitled to universal credit. If you are claiming universal credit jointly as a couple, each of you must accept an individual claimant commitment. You cannot choose to claim universal credit as a single person if your partner refuses to accept her/his claimant commitment.

You do not have to accept a claimant commitment if you do not have the capacity to do so – eg, because you have severe mental health problems and someone else (an 'appointee') is responsible for your universal credit claim. You can also be entitled to universal credit without agreeing a commitment in exceptional circumstances – eg, if there is an emergency at home or if you are in hospital.

You must accept a claimant commitment as soon as you can, and should explain to the Department for Work and Pensions (DWP) why you could not accept it earlier.

If you do not accept your claimant commitment, you may be offered a 'cooling-off period' (of no more than seven days) to think about this before a decision is made that you are not entitled to universal credit. If you are unhappy with the 'work-related requirements' you have been given, you can ask for these to be reviewed before you accept your claimant commitment. The time limit for accepting your commitment is then extended while it is reviewed.

What CPAG says

Refusing to accept a claimant commitment

If you refuse to accept your first claimant commitment and ask for it to be reviewed, you are not paid any universal credit while it is reviewed. You will only be entitled to universal credit for the period while it was being reviewed if the DWP accepts that your request was 'reasonable'. You must also accept the new claimant commitment that is offered to you or decide to accept the original claimant commitment. The universal credit regulations and guidance do not explain what 'reasonable' means. If you are asked to accept a new claimant commitment

continued $\rightarrow$

What CPAG says (continued)

when already getting universal credit and you ask for the commitment to be reviewed, your universal credit payments can be suspended while the review is carried out.

Unless your 'work coach' suggests something that is impossible for you to do, it is probably better to accept a claimant commitment and then ask for it to be reviewed after accepting the commitment. This means that you are entitled to universal credit while it is reviewed. Remember that if you do not meet the current work-related requirements in your claimant commitment while you are waiting for your review to be decided, your universal credit may be 'sanctioned', which means the amount of universal credit you receive is reduced for a period. You cannot appeal against a decision not to change your claimant commitment, but you can appeal a sanction decision.

Can you change your claimant commitment?

In practice, you may be able to discuss and agree changes to your 'claimant commitment' with your 'work coach'. However, the Department for Work and Pensions can decide when and how your commitment is updated, even if you do not agree to this. Your commitment may be updated regularly if you must look for work, as you agree different actions with your work coach. You must agree to the updated version to remain entitled to universal credit.

Your claimant commitment must be changed if there is a change in your circumstances that is relevant to which 'work-related requirements' you can be expected to do – eg, if you adopt a child or become entitled to a 'carer element' in your universal credit.

If you are unhappy with what your claimant commitment currently says you must do, you can ask your work coach for this to be reviewed. You must continue to meet your current work-related requirements while the commitment is being reviewed, otherwise your universal credit may be 'sanctioned', which reduces the amount you receive for a period. There is more information about sanctions in Chapter 7.

2. What are you expected to do?

Your 'claimant commitment' lists various things that you are expected to do in order to receive universal credit, all of which are designed to help you move into work or increase the amount of work that you do. These are known as your 'work-related requirements'.

There are different work-related requirements – the ones that apply to you depend on your circumstances. You may have to:

- look for work – this involves searching for work and being available for work
- prepare for work
- take part in 'work-focused interviews'

Some people must do all these things; others do not have any work-related requirements at all.

Use the table on p87 to identify which work-related requirements apply to you. **Note:** your partner may be in a different group to you.

If you already work, your individual work-related requirements may be reduced, depending on how much you earn and the number of hours you work.

If you do not meet your work-related requirements, your universal credit may be 'sanctioned' and the amount reduced for a period.

Box A
Main carer of a child

If you are claiming universal credit as a lone parent, you are your child(ren)'s main carer. If you are a couple claiming universal credit, you must nominate which one of you is your child(ren)'s main carer. Whoever is nominated is then the main carer for all the children in the household. You can change who is the nominated main carer, but usually only once a year unless there is a change of circumstances. If a child normally spends time in both your household and someone else's (eg, her/his other parent's household), the DWP may need to decide in which household the child 'normally lives' when deciding if you are her/his main carer.

Which work-related requirements do you have?

Your circumstances	Work-related requirements
• You are a jobseeker, or you are not in one of the groups below. • You are doing some work, you have low earnings and you are not in one of the groups below.	You have all the work-related requirements.
• You are sick or you have a disability and the Department for Work and Pensions (DWP) has assessed you as having 'limited capability for work'. • You are a lone parent or the main carer of a child aged two.	You must prepare for work and take part in work-focused interviews.
• You are a lone parent or the main carer of a child aged one. • You are a single foster carer of a child aged under 16, or the main foster carer in a couple. • You started caring for a friend's or relative's child within the past year.	You must take part in work-focused interviews.
• You are caring for a severely disabled person. • You are sick or have a disability and the DWP has assessed you as having 'limited capability for work-related activity'. • You are pregnant and expect to give birth within 11 weeks, or you have given birth within the last 15 weeks. • You are a lone parent or the main carer of a child under one. • You are the main carer of a child you have adopted within the past year. • You are at least pension age. • You are a student getting a maintenance loan or grant. • You are a young person in non-advanced education who is 'without parental support'. • You have recently experienced domestic abuse, including but not limited to domestic violence. • You are working and your earnings are sufficiently high.	You have no work-related requirements.

EXAMPLE

The main carer

Luis and Patricia have a joint claim for universal credit. Neither of them work. When their son Pablo is born (their first child), they decide to nominate Patricia as the main carer. She has no work-related requirements, and Luis must look for work. Patricia is offered a job when Pablo is six months old. She cannot take the job unless there is someone else to look after Pablo, so the couple nominate Luis as the main carer instead. Luis no longer has to look for work. Patricia is able to take the job while Luis looks after Pablo.

Who checks whether you are meeting your work-related requirements?

When you claim universal credit, a 'work coach' in your local Jobcentre Plus is usually responsible for making sure you meet your 'work-related requirements'. The work coach does not make decisions about your entitlement to universal credit; s/he focuses on what your work-related requirements should be and whether or not you have met them. If you are told to do something specific, such as attend a course or an interview, you must be notified in advance, told specifically what you must do, when you must do it and where, and the consequences if you do not do the action. This instruction might be in your 'claimant commitment' but could be by another method, such as a note in your online journal or an appointment letter.

In the longer term, the main person helping you to look or prepare for work may not be directly employed by the Department for Work and Pensions (DWP). You might be referred to the Work and Health Programme (in England and Wales), employability support in Scotland (Fair Start Scotland) or another scheme, including an unpaid work placement or a project promoting employment in a particular sector.

Although an adviser employed by one of the schemes could be the person you see most often, all the decisions about your universal credit entitlement, including whether it is 'sanctioned', are made by DWP 'decision makers'. The adviser may make recommendations to the decision maker, particularly if you have not taken part in a scheme that you received notification in advance to attend.

Proving you are meeting your work-related requirements is mainly managed online, using your online journal, but you may also be asked to attend interviews, and provide evidence and information, to show that you are meeting them.

Are your work-related requirements too harsh?

You only have the right to have your work-related requirements suspended for a period in very limited circumstances – eg, if you are recently bereaved or if you have experienced domestic violence in the last six months. However, your work coach has the discretion to reduce the hours you are expected to search for, and be available for, work to what is compatible with, or reasonable in, your circumstances. This includes your long-term circumstances (eg, if you have regular caring responsibilities or a disability) or a short-term situation – eg, if you have a domestic emergency or a sick child. DWP policy is that work coaches should use their discretion appropriately and that claimant commitments should be 'flexible and personalised'.

What CPAG says

Work-related requirements

If you think the work-related requirements in your claimant commitment are too harsh or your circumstances have changed and you should now be exempt from some or all of them, do the following.

- Make sure your work coach or adviser knows about all your individual circumstances that might affect what is in your claimant commitment.

- If your circumstances change and this might affect your ability to meet your current work-related requirements, even if only temporarily, let your work coach or adviser know as soon as possible.

continued $\longrightarrow$

What CPAG says (continued)

- Ask that your claimant commitment be reviewed if your work coach refuses to change it.

- If you have a good reason for not being able to meet any of your work-related requirements, tell your work coach or adviser as soon as possible to avoid your universal credit being 'sanctioned'.

- If your universal credit is reduced due to a sanction because you did not do something in your claimant commitment or that you were told to do by another form of notification and you think it is unreasonable, challenge the sanction decision.

3. Who must look for work?

Unless you are in one of the groups of people who have fewer 'work-related requirements', to get your full universal credit you must look for work.

To be looking for work, you must:

- search for work
- be available for work

You must also take part in 'work-focused interviews' and prepare for work, if you are asked to do so.

Coronavirus

At the start of the coronavirus pandemic, work-related requirements were suspended. During that period, you were not expected to look for work or make yourself available for work, and your universal credit could not be sanctioned if you failed to do so. From 1 July 2020, all work-related requirements can again be imposed, but your work coach should still use discretion when deciding what it is reasonable for you to do in light of ongoing coronavirus-related restrictions and disruption to the labour market.

What does 'searching for work' mean?

You must usually do anything that is reasonable to help you find work, as well as any specific actions in your 'claimant commitment' or other forms of notification. The action you take must give you the best chance of finding a job.

Box B
Searching for work

Work search may include specific activities such as:

- looking for jobs online
- applying for particular jobs
- maintaining an online profile
- registering with an employment agency
- cold-calling employers
- seeking references

When you first claim universal credit, you are usually asked to create an account on the 'Find a job' website, update your CV and create an email address, if you have not already done all these things.

Regular work search activities are then likely to include checking the 'Find a job' website and employment agency websites, contacting potential employers and applying for any specific jobs identified by your 'work coach'.

Keep as much evidence of what you have done to look for work as you can. The more evidence you have, the more likely the Department for Work and Pensions (DWP) will accept that you have been taking all reasonable steps to search for work so your universal credit will not be 'sanctioned'.

You must usually spend 35 hours a week searching for work. However, if you spend fewer hours searching for work in a week, your universal credit should not be sanctioned, provided the DWP is satisfied you took all reasonable action to find work in that week. Some people may be allowed to restrict their work search to fewer than 35 hours a week.

If this is agreed with your work coach, you are only expected to be available for work for the same number of hours. For example, if your claimant commitment says that you must spend 10 hours a week searching for work, you are only expected to be available to take up work 10 hours a week.

You may also be able to restrict your work search in other ways – eg, to the type of work or the location.

You may be able to restrict your work search if:

- you have a good work history (for the first three months of your claim)
- you have a health problem or disability
- you are caring for a child or a person with a disability

EXAMPLE

Searching for work

Samantha has been claiming universal credit and looking for work for more than four months. During this time she has registered with several employment agencies and applied for specific jobs discussed with her work coach. At a meeting to discuss Samantha's work-related requirements, her work coach decides that she needs to do a training course to make her skills more attractive to employers.

Although this is a work preparation requirement, Samantha can be asked to do this as well. Her work coach temporarily changes her claimant commitment to state that she can deduct the hours she spends on the training course from the time she must spend searching for work each week.

Do you already work?
If you are working but your earnings are low, you may be expected to search for more work. This could be by working more hours for your current employer, or taking a second job or a different job with better pay. The hours you spend at work plus your travelling time

should be deducted from the time you must spend searching for more work each week, provided your 'work coach' agrees it is reasonable to do so.

EXAMPLE

Searching for more work

Dylan is single with no caring responsibilities or health problems, so he is usually expected to spend 35 hours a week searching for work. He gets a job, working six hours on one day a week. He must drive one hour each way to get to and from work. Although he must still search for more work, he now only needs to spend 27 hours a week searching, as his work coach agrees that it is reasonable for him to deduct the eight hours he spends working and travelling.

Your universal credit can be 'sanctioned' if you do not take up more work, unless your work coach agrees that you had a good reason for refusing the work. To avoid this situation, make sure you discuss with your work coach any difficulties that taking on more work would cause you before refusing it – eg, if your current job allows you to work flexibly around your caring responsibilities but the new one would not. If your universal credit is sanctioned, you can challenge the decision and argue that you had a good reason, but there is no guarantee that your challenge will succeed.

Who does not need to search for more work?
If you are working and your gross earnings are more than a certain amount, you can no longer be required to search for work (or have any other 'work-related requirements'). That amount is called the 'earnings threshold'.

Your 'individual earnings threshold' is set at the monthly amount you would earn if you worked the equivalent number of hours that you must spend searching for work each week (usually 35) and you were paid at the national minimum wage for your age. It is less than this if you are an apprentice. The amount of your individual earnings threshold should be in your 'claimant commitment'.

Unless you have been selected for a 'pilot', the DWP currently uses a lower 'administrative' earnings threshold. If you earn above this threshold, the DWP no longer expects you to search for, or be available for, work. However, you may still be expected to take part in telephone interviews. The lower earnings threshold is the amount you would get if you were claiming jobseeker's allowance (plus the earnings disregard that would apply). In 2020/21, this is £343.85 a month for a single person and £549.47 a month for a couple.

This same threshold applies if you are self-employed and the 'minimum income floor' does not apply to you. If the minimum income floor does apply to you, you are treated as earning the amount of your individual earnings threshold (and so you have no work-related requirements), even if you actually earn less. There is more information about the minimum income floor and how your earnings are calculated if you are self-employed in Chapter 5.

If you live with a partner, in addition to your individual earnings threshold, you also have a 'joint earnings threshold'. This is your two individual earning thresholds added together. If your partner has some work-related requirements but does not have to look for work (eg, because s/he is the main carer for your two-year-old child or because s/he has been assessed as having 'limited capability for work'), s/he has a lower individual earnings threshold.

If your joint earnings are below your joint earnings threshold, both you and your partner may be expected to search for more work. If you earn more than your individual threshold, but your partner does not earn more than his/her individual threshold, however, your partner may have to search for more work while you do not. If your joint earnings are more than the joint earnings threshold, even if only one of you earns more than her/his individual threshold, neither of you need to search for more work (or have any other work-related requirements).

If you live with a partner but must claim universal credit as a single person, a joint earnings threshold still applies – it is calculated as if your partner was expected to work 35 hours a week.

The joint earnings threshold

Bob and Derek claim universal credit as a couple. They have
no children, health problems or savings and they each have an
individual earnings threshold of £1,322.53 and a joint earnings
threshold of £2,645.06. Their only other income is Derek's wages,
which are £1,000 a month before tax and national insurance.
Both Bob and Derek's claimant commitments say they must
look for more work.

Three months later, Bob finds a job paying £1,800 a month
before tax and national insurance. The couple now earn more
than their joint earnings threshold between them. Because
of this, neither of them have any work-related requirements,
even though Derek's earnings are below his individual
earnings threshold.

If your earnings vary, your average monthly earnings, before
deducting any tax or national insurance contributions, are used.
If you have a normal cycle of work, your earnings are averaged
over one cycle. If not, your earnings are normally averaged over
three months.

Do you volunteer?

If you are doing voluntary work, the number of hours that you must
spend searching for work can be reduced, provided your 'work coach'
accepts that your volunteering gives you the best chance of finding
paid work. The maximum reduction in hours is 50 per cent of what
you would otherwise spend searching for work, even if you spend
more time volunteering.

Do you have a good work history?

If you have been in work recently, for up to three months after
claiming universal credit, you may be able to restrict the type of
work you search for. This includes both the type of job and the
level of pay. This is at the discretion of your 'work coach', who

must accept that you have a reasonable chance of getting this kind of work.

> **Box C**
> **Do you have a good work history?**
>
> Whether or not you can restrict the type of job you are looking for may depend on:
>
> - the availability of the type of job you used to do
> - your prospects of getting the kind of job you had previously
> - the length of time you were employed in the same occupation
> - how long it has been since your last job ended
> - your skills and qualifications
> - training you have done for the job

Do you have a disability or health problems?

If you have a disability or a health problem, but you do not meet the conditions for having 'limited capability for work' or you are waiting for an assessment on whether you have limited capability for work, you may be able to restrict your work search. Ask that your work coach change your claimant commitment to reflect this restriction. Chapter 5 has more information about the test for limited capability for work.

You must spend what is considered a 'reasonable' amount of time each week, given your disability or health condition, searching for work. It does not matter if this restriction means that you do not have a reasonable chance of finding work.

If the DWP accepts that your disability or health has a substantial effect on your ability to carry out certain types of work, or work in a particular kind of place (eg, a dusty environment), you do not have to search for this kind of work. You may have to provide evidence of how your condition or treatment limits the type, location or hours of work for which you are searching.

If you are temporarily sick, you do not have to search for work. You can only use this rule twice a year. You can 'self-certify' as sick for up to seven days, and provide a doctor's note for a further seven days after that. If you are sick for more than 14 days, you do not have to search for work if the DWP accepts that this is reasonable. You may be asked to provide medical evidence. If you are sick for more than four weeks, the DWP may refer you for a limited capability for work assessment.

If the DWP does not accept that you cannot search for work at all, you can try to limit the kind of work you are searching for and the number of hours you are expected to search for work because of your health problems until you are assessed to see whether you have limited capability for work. Discuss what you are currently able to do with your 'work coach'.

Coronavirus

During the coronavirus pandemic, you may be treated as having limited capability for work and so should have reduced work-related requirements. For example, if you are medically advised to refrain from work due to coronavirus, you may be treated as having limited capability for work (see Chapter 5).

What CPAG says

Work-related requirements while you wait for your medical assessment

Until the DWP decides that you have limited capability for work, you can be expected to search for and be available for work, unless your work-related requirements can be reduced for another reason – eg, because you are the 'main carer' of a child under three. This is the case, even if you have 'fit notes' from your GP saying you cannot work. However, your work coach has discretion about what is reasonable for you to do, and the regulations allow her/him to reduce the hours you must search for, and be available for, work if you have a disability or health condition. You should also not need to search for, or be available for, work during the first two weeks of any period of sickness (up to two times in any 12-month period), and for longer or for

continued $\longrightarrow$

What CPAG says (continued)

additional periods at your work coach's discretion. CPAG understands that the DWP's policy is that work coaches should use this discretion appropriately when claimants are waiting to be assessed for whether they have limited capability for work. If you are in this situation, do the following.

- Self-certify for the first seven days of sickness and provide a medical certificate from your GP for any longer period.

- Ask your work coach to continue to exempt you from searching and being available for work beyond the first 14 days until your medical assessment is completed.

- If your work coach will not exempt you completely after 14 days, ask that s/he at least reduces your expected work search and availability hours to what is reasonable in light of your disability or health condition.

- If your work coach will not reduce your expected work search and availability to what is reasonable, ask for a review of your 'claimant commitment' and/or make a complaint.

- If your universal credit is 'sanctioned' because you could not meet requirements that were unreasonable, challenge the sanction on the grounds that you had a good reason.

Do you have childcare responsibilities?

If you are 'main carer' of a child aged three or younger than 13, you may be able to limit your work search to be compatible with your child's school hours (including the time taken to travel to and from school) or your childcare responsibilities if s/he has not yet started school.

Department for Work and Pensions (DWP) policy is that if the child you are responsible for is younger than 13 and in school, you can limit your work search to 25 hours per week. If the child is not yet in school, the DWP may only expect you to spend up to 16 hours a week searching for work, depending on the availability of childcare.

However, you might be able to limit the number of hours you are usually expected to spend searching for work to fewer than 25 or 16 hours depending on your individual circumstances. If you are allowed to limit the number of hours you spend searching for work every week in these circumstances, you do not need to show you still have a reasonable chance of finding a job.

You may also be able to restrict the number of hours you must spend searching for work if you sometimes look after your child who lives with your ex-partner for part of the week, or if your child is 13 or older but you need to look after her/him, perhaps because s/he has additional support needs. If the DWP accepts that you have a reasonable chance of finding work, you only have to search for work that is considered compatible with these caring responsibilities.

Do you care for someone with a disability?

If you are caring for someone who is ill or who has a disability, but you do not meet the conditions for having no 'work-related requirements' at all (eg, if you do not meet the definition of 'carer' because the cared-for person does not get a qualifying disability benefit or is waiting to hear about a claim for one), you may be able to restrict your work search. Provided the DWP accepts that you have a reasonable chance of finding work, you only have to search for work for the number of hours that are considered compatible with your caring responsibilities.

Are there any other special circumstances?

In certain circumstances, you cannot be required to search for work (or be available for work). These include if:

- your partner or child has recently died (for up to six months)
- your childcare has been disrupted
- you are carrying out certain public duties

You should explain your situation to your 'work coach' and ask for your 'claimant commitment' to be changed. However, you may still have to take part in 'work-focused interviews' or prepare for work.

In other circumstances, provided your work coach agrees that it is reasonable, your 'work-related requirements' can also be reduced. This applies if:

- you are doing training or other work preparation
- you are sick for longer than 14 days (you must provide evidence of this, if required)
- you are temporarily looking after a child
- you are dealing with a domestic emergency
- there is a temporary change in your circumstances

Even if one of the above circumstances applies, you must still search for work, be available for work and attend a job interview if your work coach thinks this would be reasonable in your particular circumstances. If you do not do so, your universal credit may be 'sanctioned' and your payments reduced. If this happens, you can challenge this decision and argue that you had a 'good reason' for failing to meet your requirements. Discuss your circumstances in advance with your work coach to avoid a sanction.

Coronavirus

During the coronavirus pandemic, it should be possible to ask your work coach to use discretion to temporarily reduce or suspend any or all of your work-related requirements if your ability to carry out any of the requirements is affected by coronavirus. A change in your circumstances during the coronavirus may mean that your work-related requirements should change – eg, you may be treated as having limited capability for work or your childcare responsibilities have increased while your children are not at school.

Have you done everything that is reasonable to search for work?
If your 'work coach' agrees that you have done everything that could reasonably be expected of you in a particular week, you have met your work search requirement, even if you spent less time searching for work than your 'claimant commitment' details. This may also be the case if you have had a temporary change in your circumstances,

such as moving house, a child being excluded from school or an emergency at home, which has meant that you have been unable to spend as long as you should have done searching for work.

What CPAG says

Hours of work search

Work coaches have the discretion to accept a reduced number of hours of work search as being reasonable. They should consider your individual circumstances and what actual work search you did in any week when deciding what is reasonable. If possible, discuss your situation in advance with your work coach and try to agree that you will look for work for a reduced number of hours. Remember that if this is not agreed, your universal credit may be 'sanctioned' if you do not stick to the hours of work search in your claimant commitment.

What does 'being available for work' mean?

'Being available for work' means that you must usually be willing and able to take up paid work immediately. This includes attending interviews in connection with obtaining work. You are expected to accept a part-time job if you are offered one, unless you have a good reason for not doing so. You must normally take any job that pays at least the national minimum wage.

Usually, you must be available immediately for any job that is within 90 minutes' travel time (each way) of your home. You must also be immediately available for job interviews within the same travel time.

If you can restrict the number of hours you spend searching for work because you are caring for a child or a disabled person, or you have a health problem or disability, you only have to be available for work for the same hours. If you have a good work history, you may be able to restrict both your work search and availability for up to three months. In some circumstances, you do not have to be available for work at all. These are the same as the circumstances when you do not need to search for work.

> **EXAMPLE**
>
> **Restricting your availability for work**
>
> Cassie is a lone parent and has a nine-year-old son. She agrees with her work coach that her expected hours of work should be 25 a week to fit in with her son's normal school hours, including the time it takes him to travel to and from school. Therefore, she only needs to be available for work during the agreed 25 hours when her son is at school.

Do you have to be available for work immediately?

You are usually expected to start work or attend a job interview immediately. There are some exceptions to this, but you must still be willing and able to start work or attend an interview at the end of the additional time you are given.

- If you are employed, you must be given 48 hours' notice to attend an interview, and you cannot be expected to take up a different job until the end of the notice period you must give to your current employer.

- If you are doing voluntary work, you may be given up to 48 hours' notice to attend an interview and up to a week's notice to start paid work, if that is considered reasonable.

- If you are caring for a child or someone with a disability, you may be given up to 48 hours' notice to attend an interview and up to a month's notice to start work, if that is considered reasonable.

4. Who must prepare for work?

Some people are not expected to look for work, but must still prepare for a future return to work. That can apply to you if you have health problems or a disability, or if you are a lone parent or the 'main carer' of a child aged two. However, if you are working and earn at least 16 times the national minimum wage, and you do not need to look for work, you do not need to prepare for work either because you no longer have any 'work-related requirements'.

If you are someone who must look for work, you can also be expected to prepare for work. This can include if you are already working but your earnings are low.

EXAMPLE

Preparing for more work when already working

Grace works two days and earns £125 a week. She is single, has no caring responsibilities, and she is not ill or disabled. She is getting universal credit and her claimant commitment says she must spend 19 hours a week trying to find another job or trying to get more hours in her current job, but after a few months she has had no luck. She would like to improve her prospects by getting new skills and so agrees with her work coach to do work experience for one day a week while continuing in her current job. Her claimant commitment is adjusted to say she will attend the work experience, continue to work and still search for more work for 10 hours a week.

Box D
Work preparation

Work preparation can include spending a set amount of time on activities, including:

- having a skills assessment
- attending a 'health and work conversation'
- improving your personal presentation
- doing training
- participating in a government employment programme
- doing work experience or unpaid work placements
- developing your own business plan

Other activities may be added to the list if your 'work coach' thinks it is necessary.

What do you *not* have to do?

Preparing for work is not the same as searching or being available for jobs. These are different 'work-related requirements'. However, you may be expected to do work experience or a work placement with an employer. If you are caring for a disabled person or a young child, you may need to explain this to your 'work coach' and ask to be given only work preparation activities that are compatible with your caring responsibilities. However, there is no right to this, and if you do not comply with the requirement, your universal credit may be 'sanctioned' unless you can show you had a good reason.

Note: participation in government employment programmes in Scotland is voluntary and so your universal credit should not be sanctioned if you do not take part in one. However, your work coach can still require you to do other work preparation and your universal credit may still be sanctioned if you do not do so.

Are you ill or do you have a disability?

If you are ill or you have a disability and are currently unfit for work, tell the Department for Work and Pensions (DWP). In some circumstances, you can be treated as having 'limited capability for work', but you usually must complete a 'work capability assessment' to decide whether your health or disability is such a serious barrier to work that you are considered to have limited capability for work. There is more information about this in Chapter 5.

If the DWP has decided you have limited capability for work, you must still prepare for work if asked to do so. If you are waiting to be assessed, or it is decided that you do not have limited capability for work and you have appealed against this decision, you must usually look for work, but your 'work coach' can reduce the amount of time you are expected to do this search to less than the full 35 hours a week if s/he considers this is reasonable.

EXAMPLE

Preparing for work

Thomas has bipolar disorder, which affects his ability to work. He is assessed as having limited capability for work but must prepare for work. Thomas used to work in an office years ago, but he is worried that his knowledge of computing will not be good enough to get a similar job when he is able to return to work.

He attends an interview with his work coach and agrees that he will attend a two-month computing course to update his skills. His work coach agrees to help him look for a one-week work placement after the course ends, so he can see how well he copes with being at work.

If you are assessed as having 'limited capability for work-related activity', rather than just limited capability for work, you do not have to prepare for work.

Are you caring for a young child?

If you are the 'main carer' of a two-year-old child, you must prepare for work. Once your youngest child reaches her/his third birthday, you may also have to search for, and be available for, work.

5. Who must take part in work-focused interviews?

Unless you have no 'work-related requirements' at all, you must take part in 'work-focused interviews'. How often you have to take part depends on your circumstances. If you are told to attend a work-focused interview and you do not do so, your universal credit can be 'sanctioned' unless you have a good reason.

If your only work-related requirement is to take part in work-focused interviews and you work and earn an amount at least 16 times the national minimum wage, you do not need to take part in work-focused interviews because you no longer have any work-related requirements.

What happens at a work-focused interview?

'Work-focused interviews' usually take place with your 'work coach' but may be with an adviser employed by an agency contracted by the Department for Work and Pensions. The purpose is to discuss how you can remain in or obtain work, including getting more work if you work already. It is not enough simply to attend a work-focused interview; you must 'take part' in the interview. Your work coach may decide that you have not taken part in your work-focused interview if, for example, you refuse to speak during the interview, only offer one-word answers or are too hungover to focus.

Box E
What is discussed at a work-focused interview?

Subjects likely to be discussed include:

- any work that you currently do, including self-employment
- how you can stay in work or increase your earnings
- your qualifications and training
- any medical condition or disability you have which may be a barrier to working
- your caring or childcare responsibilities and how they affect your ability to work
- potential work and training opportunities for the future
- accessing help and support to assist you to work

Are you caring for a young child?

If you are the 'main carer' of a child who is one year old, you must take part in 'work-focused interviews' if asked to do so. However, you cannot have any other 'work-related requirements' imposed on you.

Work-focused interviews

Anwar is the main carer for his daughter Aisha. She is one year old and is looked after by Anwar's mother every weekday morning. Anwar drops her off and picks her up, but he is able to work two hours a day during the time Aisha is with her grandmother. He thinks that he might be able to work more hours once Aisha turns three and he qualifies for a free childcare place. He must take part in work-focused interviews when asked to do so.

Even if Anwar's work coach thinks that he needs to do more to prepare for increased working hours in the future, this cannot be added to his claimant commitment until Aisha turns two.

Are you a foster carer?

There are rules for registered foster carers who have a child placed with them. If you are looking after a friend's or relative's child who is 'looked after' by the local authority (often referred to as 'kinship care'), you may be treated as a foster carer under these rules.

If you are a single foster carer or the 'main carer' in a couple, you must take part in 'work-focused interviews' but have no other 'work-related requirements' from your foster child's first birthday until s/he turns 16.

If your partner is not the main carer, s/he usually has the work-related requirements that are appropriate for her/his circumstances.

You must attend work-focused interviews, but have no other work-related requirements, if you are the main carer of a foster child aged 16 to 19 who has extra care needs, or if your partner is the main carer but you both need to care for your foster child because of the level of her/his care needs. The Department for Work and Pensions must accept that it is reasonable for you not to have to look for work, even for a limited number of hours a week.

If you are between fostering placements, you do not have any additional work-related requirements for the first eight weeks after your last placement ended, provided you intend to continue fostering.

Are you looking after a child of a friend or relative?

If you are the 'main carer' of a child of any age whose parents have died or who are unable to look after her/him, you must take part in 'work-focused interviews', but you have no other 'work-related requirements', during the first year after you become the child's main carer. This also applies during the first year of looking after a child who would otherwise be taken into care.

If the child is being 'looked after' by the local authority, you may instead be treated as a foster carer and have no other work-related requirements until s/he turns 16.

6. Who has no work-related requirements?

In certain circumstances, you cannot be asked to meet any 'work-related requirements' to get universal credit. However, you must still accept a 'claimant commitment'.

If you are working and your earnings are sufficiently high, you cannot be asked to meet any work-related requirements.

Are you caring for a person with a severe disability?

You have no 'work-related requirements' if you get a 'carer element' in your universal credit. You get this if you care for a severely disabled person for at least 35 hours a week, and no one else gets a carer element for caring for the same person. You do not count as a carer under these rules if you are providing paid care or if you are in full-time education.

The definition of who is a 'severely disabled person' is linked to the rate of disability living allowance, personal independence payment or attendance allowance received by the person for whom you care.

If you do not qualify for the carer element, but you spend 35 hours or more a week caring for one or more severely disabled people, you may still not have any work-related requirements. However, this decision is at the discretion of the Department for Work and Pensions. It must accept that it would be unreasonable for you to look for any work at all, even for a limited number of hours.

There is more information about universal credit and carers in Chapter 10.

Are you older than pension age?

If you are older than pension age (currently around age 66 for both women and men and gradually increasing to 68) and you get universal credit as a couple because you live with a younger partner, you have no 'work-related requirements'. Your partner may have work-related requirements. There is more information about older people and universal credit in Chapter 10.

Are you pregnant or caring for a child younger than one?

If you are pregnant and your baby is due in 11 weeks or fewer, or you gave birth within the last 15 weeks, you have no 'work-related requirements'.

In addition, if you are either a lone parent or the 'main carer' in a couple and have a child aged under one included as part of your family in your universal credit award, or you are fostering a child under one, you have no work-related requirements.

If you are a couple claiming universal credit, you must nominate which one of you is your child(ren)'s main carer. Whoever is nominated is then the main carer for all the children in the household. Couples with a new baby can therefore nominate the mother's partner as the main carer of all their children, so s/he can help with childcare around the time of the birth without having to worry about meeting any work-related requirements. You must decide who to nominate from 15 weeks after your baby is born – from this date the mother no longer automatically has no work-related requirements.

You can change who is the nominated main carer but if you want to do so more than once a year, that is at the discretion of the Department for Work and Pensions. You should therefore discuss your plans with your 'work coach' in advance. If your work-related requirements are not reduced, you should continue to meet them and ask for your 'claimant commitment' to be reviewed, as otherwise your universal credit may be 'sanctioned'.

Have you recently adopted a child?

If you are the 'main carer' of a child with whom you have been matched for adoption, you have no 'work-related requirements' for one year after the child is placed with you. If you want, you can choose that this period start up to two weeks before the child is placed with you. These rules do not apply if you were a foster parent or close relative of the child before adopting her/him.

Are you severely ill or do you have a severe disability?

If the Department for Work and Pensions has decided that you have 'limited capability for work-related activity', you have no 'work-related requirements'.

There is more information about the assessment for limited capability for work-related activity in Chapter 5.

Are you a student?

If you are a full-time student eligible for universal credit and you receive a grant, bursary or loan that is taken into account as income, you have no 'work-related requirements'. **Note:** most students are not eligible to claim universal credit.

You have no work-related requirements during the months in which your student income is taken into account when calculating your universal credit award, so you may still have some work-related requirements during the long summer vacation.

You also do not have any work-related requirements if you are a young student in non-advanced education and you can claim universal credit because you do not get any parental support.

Have you recently experienced domestic abuse or violence?

Even if you would normally have to meet some (or all) of the 'work-related requirements', you do not have to do so for 13 weeks if you have recently experienced domestic violence. You must no longer live with the perpetrator and you must tell the Department for Work and Pensions (DWP) within six months of the abuse. Within one month of notifying the DWP, you must provide evidence that the abuse is likely to have occurred. This must be from one of a list of professionals, including a police officer or social worker.

You can only be exempted from your work-related requirements once in any one-year period under this rule.

If you are the 'main carer' of a child and would normally have to look for work at the end of this 13-week period, you cannot be required to look for work for a further 13 weeks. However, you can be required to take part in 'work-focused interviews' or prepare for work.

The definition of 'domestic violence' includes controlling or coercive behaviour or actual or threatened physical, financial, psychological, emotional or sexual abuse, where the perpetrator was either your partner or certain other relatives.

Further information

On gov.uk there is *Advice for Decision Making*, produced by the Department for Work and Pensions for its own staff. Chapters J1 to J3 explain the claimant commitment and work-related requirements.

There is more information on the work-related requirements that apply to universal credit in CPAG's *Welfare Benefits and Tax Credits Handbook*.

Chapter 7
Sanctions and fines

This chapter covers:

1. When can your universal credit be sanctioned?

2. When can your universal credit not be sanctioned?

3. How much is a sanction and how long does it last?

4. When can you get a hardship payment?

5. When can you be fined?

6. What happens to your universal credit after a benefit offence?

What you need to know

- If you do not meet your 'work-related requirements', the amount of your universal credit can be reduced. That is called a 'sanction'. The sanction can last indefinitely or for a set period. Your universal credit should not be sanctioned if you have a good reason for not meeting a requirement.

- If you cannot meet your basic needs because of a sanction, you may be able to get a 'hardship payment'. That is a loan, which you may have to repay.

- If you are overpaid universal credit because you did not provide information promptly or you gave incorrect information, you may be given a 'civil penalty'.

- If you give false information or act dishonestly in relation to your claim and there may be grounds to prosecute you for fraud, you may be able to accept a fine instead of being prosecuted. If you accept a fine or are convicted of fraud, your universal credit can also be reduced.

1. When can your universal credit be sanctioned?

If you do not meet a specific 'work-related requirement' that you have previously been told you must complete in your 'claimant commitment' or by another form of notification, your universal credit can be reduced unless you have a good reason for acting as you did. That is called a 'sanction'. The amount of the sanction and how long it lasts depends on which work-related requirements apply to you and the reason for the sanction.

Coronavirus

During the coronavirus pandemic, the Department for Work and Pensions (DWP) has relaxed some of the rules around work-related requirements, so your universal credit is less likely to be sanctioned. See Chapter 6 for more details. The DWP has also said that during the coronavirus outbreak it will only impose sanctions as a last resort, although pre-existing sanctions will continue. That is likely to change as the government's response and rules about what you are allowed to do during the coronavirus outbreak change. This may also depend on where you live in the UK. Your universal credit can still be sanctioned for something you did before claiming, such as leaving a job voluntarily, as those rules have not been relaxed.

Do you have to look for work?

If you have to look for work as a condition of getting universal credit, your universal credit may be 'sanctioned' if you do not do something specific that is set out in your 'claimant commitment' or something else you have been specifically told you must do in some other form of notification – eg in a note on your online journal. There are three levels of sanctions.

A **high-level** sanction can be applied to your universal credit if:

- You do not apply for a specific job.
- You do not take up a job offer, even if this was before you claimed universal credit.

- You give up a job or lose pay voluntarily or because of misconduct, even if this was before you claimed universal credit.

A **medium-level** sanction can be applied to your universal credit if:

- You are not available to start work or attend a job interview as set out in your claimant commitment.
- You are not doing enough to find work.

A **low-level** sanction can be applied to your universal credit if:

- You do not undertake any of your other specific work search or work preparation requirements, such as updating your CV or attending a training or employability course.
- You do not participate in a 'work-focused interview'.
- You do not report a change of circumstances, provide information or attend an interview about your 'work-related requirements'.

EXAMPLES

Sanctions if you must look for work

Mandy lives alone and has no health problems. She gives up her job because she finds it boring and claims universal credit. The Department for Work and Pensions does not accept that Mandy had a good reason for leaving her job and applies a high-level sanction to her universal credit for 91 days.

Eric and Freya claim universal credit as a couple and are both looking for work. Freya misses an interview for a course that her work coach told her to attend. A low-level sanction is applied to their universal credit because she failed to attend an interview about work preparation.

Do you **not** have to look for work?

Even if you do not have to look for work, your universal credit may be 'sanctioned' if you do not do something specific that is in your 'claimant commitment' or that you have previously been notified you must do by some other means – eg, on an appointment card. There are two levels of sanctions.

A **low-level** sanction can be applied to your universal credit if you are expected both to prepare for work and attend 'work-focused interviews', and, for instance:

- You do not take up a work placement you are told to do.
- You do not participate in a suitable training course identified by your 'work coach'.
- You do not take part in a work-focused interview.
- You do not report a change in your circumstances that affects your 'work-related requirements'.

Only a **lowest level** sanction can be applied to your universal credit if you are expected to attend work-focused interviews (but have no other work-related requirements) and you do not participate in such an interview.

EXAMPLE

Sanctions if you do not have to look for work

Joachim is unable to work because of his mental health problems, but he is expected to prepare for work, including taking up work placements. His work coach finds him a work placement that she thinks is suitable. On the day the placement begins, Joachim forgets to set his alarm and misses the introductory session. A low-level sanction is applied to his universal credit.

Do you disagree with a decision to sanction your universal credit?

If your universal credit is 'sanctioned' when you do not think it should have been, you can challenge that decision. You may have a good reason for not meeting a particular requirement. Your 'work-related requirements' may be unreasonable or you might not have been properly notified in advance about what you needed to do. You can also challenge the decision if you think the wrong level, length or amount of sanction has been applied.

You must first ask the Department for Work and Pensions to look at the decision again (called a 'mandatory reconsideration'). If you remain unhappy, you can appeal to an independent tribunal. Chapter 9 has more information on challenging decisions.

2. When can your universal credit not be sanctioned?

You can take steps to reduce the chances of the Department for Work and Pensions (DWP) 'sanctioning' your universal credit. In some situations, your universal credit should not be sanctioned.

You can avoid a sanction by understanding what is expected of you as a condition of your getting universal credit. The general requirements should be set out in your 'claimant commitment', but more specific actions may be in other information you have received, such as a letter about an interview or an email giving instructions about when and where to attend a work placement. There is more information on this in Chapter 6. Make sure that the DWP understands your current circumstances, so that you are only expected to undertake the relevant 'work-related requirements' and your claimant commitment reflects these.

Note: in Scotland, employability programmes are voluntary. If you have been referred to a Scottish employability scheme ('Fair Start Scotland'), you should not be given a sanction if you choose not to participate. You must still keep to any other work-related requirements in your claimant commitment or other forms of notification, otherwise you risk your universal credit being sanctioned.

What CPAG says

Avoiding sanctions

- Remember, you are not expected to meet all the possible work-related requirements in certain circumstances – eg, if you are caring for a young child or a person with a severe disability.

- Your 'work coach' may agree it is reasonable to limit the number of hours you are expected to search for work or be available for work – eg, if you have a child under 13 in school or if you already have a part-time job.

- If you are finding it hard to do everything in your claimant commitment or you think a condition is unreasonable, ask for it to be reviewed.

- Keep a written or online record of everything you do to look for or prepare for work and take it to any interviews with your work coach.

- If your circumstances change, report the change immediately, as your claimant commitment may need to be amended.

- Some, or all, of the conditions in your claimant commitment must be suspended in certain circumstances – eg, if you are bereaved or sick for a short period. Inform your work coach as soon as possible.

- If you are expected to apply for a particular job or attend an interview or a course or placement, you should receive notification and full details in advance, including what will happen if you do not do it – ie, that your universal credit may be sanctioned. If you have not, your universal credit cannot be sanctioned for you not doing the requirement.

- Try to stick to the work-related requirements in your claimant commitment and any specific actions you are notified of, but if you have a good reason for not keeping to them, let your work coach know as soon as possible.

continued →

What CPAG says (continued)

- If you do not do exactly what it says in your claimant commitment or another notification, check whether you did something else that still meets your work-related requirements – eg, you did not register with two employment agencies as required because you found out that a local employer had new vacancies, so you applied for one instead.

- If you are in work but your earnings are low, a sanction should only be given as a last resort.

EXAMPLE

Avoiding a sanction

Marshall has recently started claiming universal credit after being made redundant. His claimant commitment says that he is expected to search for work 35 hours a week and be available for work immediately. However, he has main responsibility for his nine-year-old daughter and can only be available for work and look for work while she is at school. He is struggling to show that he is meeting all his work-related requirements. At an interview with his work coach, she agrees that it is reasonable for him to restrict the number of hours he is expected to search and be available for work. His claimant commitment is changed to say that he must search for work and be available for 20 hours a week.

Do you have a good reason?

In most cases, if you can show that you had a good reason for not meeting a requirement or carrying out a specific action, your universal credit is not 'sanctioned'.

'Good reason' is not defined in the rules, but there is guidance about the kinds of circumstances that can be taken into account. As well as general factors, there may be other specific circumstances in your case. For example, you may have a good reason not to apply for a job if the cost of your childcare or travel will make up an unreasonably high proportion of the pay.

The Department for Work and Pensions (DWP) should consider all your circumstances and then decide whether or not you have a good reason.

When making this decision, the DWP normally uses information from your 'work coach', as s/he may have asked for a decision on whether your universal credit should be sanctioned. Information from agencies that are providing you with day-to-day work-related support, such as your work placement or course supervisor, may also be important, so make sure they are informed of your circumstances and any changes. Also, make sure you give your own explanation and keep a record of who you have told and when.

Box A
What is a good reason?

Examples of what may be relevant when deciding whether or not you have a good reason include:

- there is a domestic emergency
- you have a mental health condition
- you have a disability
- you have a learning disability
- you are homeless
- you have experienced domestic violence
- you have experienced bullying or harassment
- you have caring responsibilities
- you refused to accept a zero-hour contract which excludes you from taking other work
- you have been sick
- you have transport problems
- you have problems with your post
- your internet access is disrupted
- undertaking the requirement would cause you harm
- you have legitimate health and safety concerns

EXAMPLE

Good reason

Terry is made redundant after doing the same job for 15 years. At an interview just after he claims universal credit, his work coach identifies a similar job with a different employer, which is being advertised on the 'Find a job' website. The work coach adds a note to Terry's online universal credit journal telling him to apply by the closing date or risk having a high-level sanction applied to his universal credit.

Before applying, Terry contacts the employer for more details. The job is not based at the main office, which means Terry would be working a long way from home, and the train fares would cost him almost half of the salary on offer. Terry explains this to his work coach and it is accepted that he has a good reason for not applying for the job. His universal credit is not sanctioned.

Have you stopped working or lost earnings voluntarily or because of misconduct?

If you stop working or change your hours so that you lose earnings, your universal credit may be 'sanctioned'. Your universal credit should only be sanctioned if you have either done that voluntarily and you do not have a good reason or it has happened because of your misconduct.

The words 'voluntarily' and 'misconduct' are not defined in any special way. Box B lists some issues to bear in mind.

Box B
What is misconduct?

- Being careless or negligent, or refusing to do something without a good reason might be misconduct if it is serious enough. Being dismissed for poor performance is not necessarily misconduct.

- Misconduct must normally be connected with your employment in some way, although it does not necessarily need to happen while you are working.

- Dishonesty is misconduct if it means that your employer does not trust you and dismisses you because of dishonesty.

- Being persistently late or being off sick without explanation might be misconduct.

- If you resign to avoid being dismissed, that can count as misconduct.

- If your employer says you were dismissed because of misconduct but is really just reducing staff numbers, that should not count as misconduct.

Your universal credit should not be sanctioned in certain circumstances.

- You are made redundant or take voluntary redundancy.
- You leave or lose pay as a member of the armed forces, even if you left voluntarily.
- You have been laid off or put on short-time working by your employer.
- You leave a job or lose pay while still in a trial period.
- You are involved in a trade dispute.
- You leave a job or lose pay, but your weekly earnings do not fall below your 'individual earnings threshold' (see Chapter 6).

3. How much is a sanction and how long does it last?

If your universal credit is 'sanctioned', the amount you are paid is usually reduced. The most it can be reduced by is an amount equal to the adult 'standard allowance' that applies to you. If you are claiming as a couple and only one of you has your universal credit sanctioned, the maximum reduction is half your standard allowance as a couple. In some cases, a lower rate applies.

A sanction can last for an indefinite period or for a set number of days. A sanction starts from the beginning of the monthly 'assessment period' in which the Department for Work and Pensions makes the sanction decision, not when you did (or failed to do) whatever the sanction is being applied for.

How much is a sanction?

The amount of a 'sanction' is worked out on a daily basis and depends on your age and whether you are single or in a couple. The amount that applies is then deducted from your universal credit award for each day in the 'sanction period'.

The 'usual' sanction rate applies, unless at the end of the 'assessment period' in which the reduction is being made one of the following applies – in which case, the lower rate applies:

- your only 'work-related requirement' is to attend 'work-focused interviews'
- you are aged 16 or 17
- you are a lone parent or 'main carer' for a child under one
- you are pregnant and within 11 weeks of when you expect to give birth
- you have given birth in the last 15 weeks
- you have had an adopted child placed with you within the last year

The amount of the sanction may be the same as, or more than, the amount of your universal credit award. If that is the case, you are paid no universal credit for the period of the sanction.

Daily rate of sanction, 2020/21

	Usual rate	Lower rate
Single, under 25	£11.20	£4.40
Single, 25 or over	£13.40	£5.30
Couple, both under 25 (per person sanctioned)	£8.00	£3.20
Couple, at least one aged 25 or older (per person sanctioned)	£9.70	£3.80

EXAMPLE

The amount of a sanction

Duncan is 43, single and unemployed. His work coach notifies him of a job vacancy, but Duncan does not apply for it because his mother is taken into hospital. He is given a sanction for 91 days. The sanction is applied for the whole of his monthly assessment periods for April, May and June.

His usual universal credit award is £709.89 a month, made up of £409.89 standard allowance and £300 housing costs. The sanction is £402 in April and June (30 days x £13.40) and £409.89 for May (31 days x £13.40, limited to the amount of his standard allowance).

He gets paid about £300 a month for those three months, just enough to cover his rent, but not enough for bills or food. Duncan does three things.

- He contacts his work coach to explain his reasons for not applying for the vacancy.

- He asks an advice centre for help challenging the sanction.

- He applies for a hardship payment.

If you are sanctioned, you may find that you are left without enough money to cover your basic needs, such as food and bills. If that is the case, you can apply for a hardship payment.

How long does a sanction last?

Length of sanctions

Level of sanction	Length of sanction		
	First failure	Second failure within a year	Third or further failure within a year
High level – eg, you failed to apply for a job	91 days	182 days	182 days
Medium level – eg, you failed to take all reasonable action to get work	28 days	91 days	91 days
Low level – eg, you failed to take particular action to prepare for work	Until you comply plus seven days after that	Until you comply plus 14 days after that	Until you comply plus 28 days after that
Lowest level – eg, you failed to attend a 'work-focused interview'	Until you comply	Until you comply	Until you comply

The number of days a 'sanction' lasts usually depends on the level of sanction and whether your universal credit has been sanctioned at the same level before. If your universal credit has been sanctioned for something you did before you claimed, another sanction should not be for a longer period. For example, if you left your last job voluntarily before claiming universal credit and a 91-day high-level sanction was applied, and you then fail to apply for a job within a year, the new high-level sanction is also for 91 days. The length of sanction also does not increase if another sanction of the same level is applied for something you did within 14 days of the previous 'failure'. For example, your work coach decides you did not take all reasonable action to search for work in a week and so a 28-day medium-level sanction is applied to your universal credit, and if the work coach decides you also did not take all reasonable action again in the following week, another 28-day sanction will be applied, not a 91-day sanction.

Sometimes, the length of a sanction depends on the time between your failing to do something and when you comply with the particular 'work-related requirement', rather than for a set period.

Any sanction is applied from the beginning of the 'assessment period' in which the Department for Work and Pensions decides to sanction your universal credit – not from when you did, or did not do, whatever the sanction has been applied for. That may mean that your universal credit carries on being sanctioned even though you have now complied with the requirement the sanction was applied for failing to do.

EXAMPLE

Length of a sanction

Jerry's assessment period runs from the 14th to the 13th of each month. He has limited capability for work and so is required to prepare for work. On 18 October a low-level sanction is applied to his universal credit because on 28 September he did not attend a training course his work coach found for him and he did not have a good reason for failing to attend. This is Jerry's first universal credit sanction. The length of the sanction is open-ended until he complies with his work-related requirements.

Jerry immediately contacts his work coach and they agree that if he attends a different course, starting on 25 October, he will be treated as having met the original requirement. He starts the course as agreed and has a 35-day sanction (28 September to 25 October = 28 days + a fixed seven days for a first low-level sanction) applied from the start of his current assessment period – ie, 14 October to 13 November. The sanction period will end on 17 November.

Shorter sanction periods apply to 16/17 year olds.

If your universal credit is already being sanctioned and another sanction is applied, the new sanction starts when the current one ends. This means having another sanction applied when one is already in place results in a longer sanction period rather than a higher daily rate of sanction. However, you cannot have more than a total of 1,095 days of sanctions applied to your universal credit at any one time.

What happens if your circumstances change?

The 'sanction period' continues, even if your universal credit award ends. If you reclaim universal credit before the sanction period ends, the sanction continues for the remainder of the period.

If, since the start of the last sanction, you have been in work for six months and earning at least a certain amount (known as your 'individual earnings threshold'), any remaining sanctions on your universal credit award are written off. Time spent in different jobs with gaps in between can count towards the six months.

The daily amount of a sanction is reduced to zero (ie, you get your full universal credit entitlement) if you are assessed as having 'limited capability for work-related activity' and so you have no 'work-related requirements'. There is more information about this assessment in Chapter 5. The sanction period still continues, however, so that if your health improves before the sanction period ends, deductions can start again.

If your circumstances change which mean that you are now a person to whom the lower/usual rate applies, the daily amount of the sanction also changes from the start of the 'assessment period' in which your circumstances change.

> **EXAMPLE**
>
> **Change of circumstances**
>
> Belle's universal credit has a second high-level sanction of 182 days applied after she left a job voluntarily while getting universal credit and then did not take up an offer of a suitable new job within a year. Eight weeks (56 days) after the start of the sanction period, she gets a new job. Her earnings mean that she no longer qualifies for universal credit, so her award stops. However, Belle's new job ends after three months (92 days) as the company goes into administration, and she reclaims universal credit immediately. The sanction continues and her new award of universal credit continues to be reduced for a further 34 days.

4. When can you get a hardship payment?

If your universal credit is reduced because of a 'sanction', you may be able to get a 'hardship payment'. These are loans and are usually recovered from your universal credit once the sanction period ends. You can only apply for a hardship payment if your universal credit has been reduced because of a sanction (including if it is sanctioned for benefit fraud). Hardship payments are not paid if you are in hardship for any other reason.

If your universal credit is reduced by the lower or nil sanction rate in an 'assessment period', you cannot get a hardship payment to cover the reduction in your benefit for that assessment period. That is because the sanction has not reduced your universal credit by the full amount of the 'standard allowance'.

To get a hardship payment, you must be unable to meet your or your partner's or child's immediate basic needs. These are your:

- accommodation
- heating
- food
- hygiene

You may need to show that you have tried to access other sources of support, such as help from relatives, but you should not be expected to go to a food bank first. You may also have to show that you have tried to stop any non-essential spending.

To get a hardship payment, you must apply in the assessment period in which you have received the reduced amount of universal credit and provide any required information. You must also continue to meet your 'work-related requirements'. It is important that you explain your circumstances when you apply for a hardship payment. The Department for Work and Pensions is more likely to accept that you need one if, for example, you have children or caring responsibilities, or if you are ill or pregnant, or if your universal credit has already been sanctioned for some time.

You can appeal if you are refused a hardship payment.

How much are hardship payments and how long do they last?

'Hardship payments' are paid at 60 per cent of the daily amount by which your universal credit has been reduced. They are usually paid for the number of days between when you apply and when you are due to get your next regular payment of universal credit. However, if your next regular universal credit payment is in less than eight days, they are paid until the *following* regular universal credit payment – ie, for up to 38 days.

For example, if you are a single person older than 25 and your universal credit is sanctioned for 14 days so that your monthly universal credit is reduced by £187.60, the daily rate of your hardship payments is £3.70 (£187.60 x 12, divided by 365, x 60 per cent). If hardship payments are awarded for the 27 days before your next regular payment of universal credit, you will receive £99.90.

As a hardship payment is usually paid for the period until your next universal credit payment is due, you must then apply again the following month – ie, for each new 'assessment period' in which you have received a reduced amount of universal credit.

When do you repay a hardship payment?

Once the 'sanction period' is over, you must usually repay the 'hardship payment'. Your universal credit award is reduced by a set amount until the payment is repaid, in the same way as if you were repaying an overpayment of universal credit (see Chapter 8). However, sometimes you do not need to repay a hardship payment, either at all or for a period.

• You do not need to repay a hardship payment while you are working and earning at least a certain amount (known as your 'individual earnings threshold').

• If you are working and have been earning at least your individual earnings threshold for a total of six months since any sanctions ended, any hardship payment you have not yet repaid is written off completely.

EXAMPLE

Hardship payments

Anita and Tony have two children, aged six and eight. Tony resigned from his job and they have claimed universal credit as a couple. Their universal credit is sanctioned, as the Department for Work and Pensions (DWP) decides Tony left his job without a good reason. He is looking for work. Anita is pregnant and unwell because of complications in her pregnancy. They have no other income. They explain their circumstances to their work coach and provide evidence to show that they cannot meet their essential needs, have no non-essential expenditure and have not been able to get help from other members of their family. The DWP decides that they can get a hardship payment of universal credit.

Tony then finds a new job. As it pays enough, the recovery of their hardship payments is suspended and, after six months, they are written off.

Tony can also appeal against the sanction decision. He may have good reason for leaving his job if it was due to Anita's pregnancy and illness, together with the needs of their children.

5. When can you be fined?

There are two types of benefit fines that the Department for Work and Pensions (DWP) can give you while you are getting universal credit.

- You can be given a fine (known as a 'civil penalty') if you are overpaid universal credit because of something that you have done or failed to do.

- If there may be grounds to prosecute you for fraud, you may be offered the option of accepting a fine (known as an 'administrative penalty') instead of being prosecuted.

Get advice immediately if you are being prosecuted for benefit fraud, have been offered a fine to avoid the possibility of being prosecuted, or have been asked to attend a formal interview 'under caution'.

Coronavirus

During the coronavirus pandemic, you may have claimed universal credit for the first time and not had any face-to-face contact with DWP staff while doing so. This means that the DWP may not have been as thorough in checking all of your circumstances or asking for all the information and evidence they usually require when someone makes a new claim. You may also have found it difficult to contact DWP to report any changes that might affect your new or existing universal credit award. If it later turns out that you were overpaid or not entitled at all to universal credit during the coronavirus outbreak because of that, provided you answered all questions honestly and provided all the information that was correct to the best of your knowledge at the time, you should not be fined or threatened with prosecution for fraud.

Have you been overpaid?

You can be given a 'civil penalty' of £50 if you have been overpaid universal credit by at least £65.01. The overpayment must have occurred because:

- you 'negligently' made an incorrect statement
- you 'negligently' provided incorrect information or evidence
- you failed to report a relevant change of circumstances 'without a reasonable excuse'

In the first two cases, you are not given a penalty if you have taken 'reasonable steps' to correct your error.

What 'negligently', 'reasonable excuse' and 'reasonable steps' mean is not defined in the universal credit rules. The Department for Work and Pensions (DWP), therefore, has to decide whether you have acted 'negligently' or have taken 'reasonable steps' to correct an error, or have a 'reasonable excuse' for not reporting a change of circumstances. It has guidance to help it make these decisions. For example, you might not be fined if you have a learning disability and you did not understand what you were doing.

EXAMPLE

Civil penalty

Nigel works part time. His daughter Clara attends nursery while he works and he receives help towards the costs of childcare in his universal credit. Nigel decides that he wants to spend more time with Clara, reorganises his work and reduces her childcare by a few hours a week. He mistakenly reports the wrong amount of childcare costs for two months. The DWP decides that Nigel has acted negligently, but that the situation is not sufficiently serious to prosecute him for fraud. Nigel's universal credit award is amended, an overpayment of £180 is calculated and a £50 penalty is added to it.

Nigel can appeal against the decision to add a penalty to his overpayment if he thinks he did not act negligently and/or took reasonable steps to correct his error.

You can only be given a civil penalty if you have not been charged with an offence or offered the choice of accepting an 'administrative penalty' in connection with the same overpayment.

If you disagree with the decision to give you a civil penalty, including if you think the overpayment was not worked out correctly, you may be able to appeal.

Your partner cannot be fined if s/he was unaware of your negligence, or if s/he has a reasonable excuse for not providing the information needed.

Are there grounds to prosecute you for fraud?

If the Department for Work and Pensions (DWP) thinks there are grounds to prosecute you for a benefit fraud offence, you may be offered a fine (an 'administrative penalty') instead. If you accept this fine, you cannot be prosecuted for the same offence but your universal credit can still be 'sanctioned' for a period.

If you are being offered a fine, you are invited to an interview to discuss it. You can be given up to five days afterwards to decide whether to accept it, provided the DWP thinks this is reasonable.

If you accept the fine, you have 14 days to change your mind. If you withdraw your acceptance, the DWP must refund any of the fine you have already paid, but may decide to prosecute you instead.

If you accept a penalty as an alternative to being prosecuted, the amount you are fined is:

- £350 if there has been no overpayment
- 50 per cent of the overpayment, subject to a minimum of £350 and a maximum of £5,000

What CPAG says

Accepting a fine

If the DWP offers you a fine, it may be difficult to decide what to do. On the one hand, if you accept the fine you avoid prosecution. On the other hand, you must pay the fine and your universal credit may also be reduced ('sanctioned') for a period. Always get independent advice to help you decide.

> **EXAMPLE**
>
> **Penalty instead of prosecution**
>
> Aaron claims universal credit for himself and his two children. Before any payment is made, his claim is turned down, as the DWP believes the children live with his ex-wife Maria, who already gets universal credit for them. Aaron has not provided any evidence of when the children stay with him. Although no overpayment has been made to Aaron, the DWP believes that he deliberately claimed for the children dishonestly in order to get more benefit, and so he could be prosecuted for fraud. Rather than start proceedings, Aaron is offered the alternative of paying a £350 fine. He should get advice before accepting this.
>
> Depending on the children's living arrangements, Aaron may be able to argue that he can claim for the children. To be convicted, the DWP must prove that Aaron knew he was not entitled to amounts of universal credit for them and was acting dishonestly.

How do you pay a fine?

A fine is recoverable from you in the same way as an overpayment of universal credit. There is more information about overpayments and how they are recovered in Chapter 8.

If you have a joint universal credit claim, the fine is recovered from your joint award. It may also be recovered by other methods (eg, by deductions from other benefits or from earnings) from you or from your partner.

If a fine is being recovered from you and the decision that you have been overpaid is later changed (eg, if your appeal against the overpayment decision is successful), the Department for Work and Pensions must refund any amount of the fine that you have already paid.

6. What happens to your universal credit after a benefit offence?

If you are convicted of a benefit offence or you accept a fine to avoid possible prosecution, your universal credit can also be 'sanctioned' for a set period of time. This usually means that you are paid less universal credit but, in some cases, it can mean losing entitlement altogether. You can apply for a 'hardship payment' in the same way as when your universal credit is sanctioned for not meeting your 'work-related requirements'.

The sanction lasts for four weeks if you accept a penalty instead of prosecution. If you are prosecuted and convicted and it is your first offence, the sanction usually lasts for 13 weeks. If you are convicted again for another benefit offence, the sanction period is longer.

EXAMPLE

Sanction for a benefit offence

Connor accepts a fine of 50 per cent of the amount of an overpayment of universal credit as an alternative to being prosecuted, after it was found that he had not declared the casual work he had been doing. As well as the fine, his universal credit is sanctioned for four weeks.

Further information

The official guidance about sanctions and hardship payments is in the DWP's *Advice for Decision Making* at gov.uk/government/publications/advice-for-decision-making-staff-guide.
There is also more information about sanctions, fraud and penalties in CPAG's *Welfare Benefits and Tax Credits Handbook* and on the AskCPAG website.

Chapter 8
Overpayments

This chapter covers:

1. What happens if you are overpaid?

2. Do you have to repay an overpayment?

3. How do you repay an overpayment?

What you need to know

- If you are overpaid universal credit, the Department for Work and Pensions (DWP) can recover the money, even if the overpayment was caused by its own mistake.

- You can appeal if you think you were not overpaid or the amount is wrong, but you cannot appeal against a decision to recover an overpayment.

- You can ask the DWP not to recover an overpayment, but it is only likely to agree in exceptional circumstances.

- The DWP usually recovers an overpayment from your ongoing award of universal credit, but may recover it in other ways, including from your earnings.

- You can ask the DWP to reduce the repayments if they are causing hardship or affecting your family's health or welfare.

1. What happens if you are overpaid?

If more universal credit is paid to you than you are entitled to, you have been overpaid.

There are many reasons why universal credit might be overpaid, including the following.

- You give the wrong information when you claim.

- You are late reporting a change of circumstances.

- Your employer gives the wrong details about your earnings when reporting these to HM Revenue and Customs (HMRC).

- The Department for Work and Pensions (DWP) makes a mistake when it works out your award or when it records the information you give.

- The DWP does not act on the information you give.

- The DWP does not pass on information from one department to another.

EXAMPLES

Why overpayments happen

Parveen is working part time. Her employer has mixed up the details of her earnings with those of someone else and has told HMRC that she earns less than she does. When the mistake comes to light, the DWP revises her award. She has an overpayment of universal credit.

Wayne claims universal credit when he stops work because of cancer treatment. His partner moves in to look after him. He does not realise that he needs to inform the DWP. When he does tell the DWP some months later, he finds he has an overpayment of universal credit as Wayne and his partner should have claimed as a couple.

Anna has an award of universal credit of £300 a month. One month, there is a mix-up in the system and two sums of £300 are paid into her bank account on the same day by mistake. Anna queries it and is told that this is an overpayment.

If your universal credit is overpaid, the DWP should do the following.

- **Change the decision.** If the overpayment is because of a change in your entitlement to universal credit, the DWP must usually 'revise' or 'supersede' the decision awarding you benefit. These are the legal ways in which the DWP can change a decision on your entitlement. In some circumstances, the DWP does not have to change the decision before recovering an overpayment – eg, if you are paid twice by mistake or if someone else receives a payment intended for you.

- **Calculate the amount of the overpayment.** This is usually the difference between what you were paid and how much you should have been entitled to.

- **Decide whether or not to recover the overpayment.** The DWP can recover any overpayment, even when it is not your fault. However, it has discretion about whether or not to do so.

- **Decide who to recover the overpayment from.** The general rule is that an overpayment can be recovered from the person to whom it was paid. If you claim jointly as a couple, it can be recovered from one or both of you, even if you are not the one who received the payment.

- **Decide how to recover the overpayment.** There are various methods the DWP can use to recover an overpayment.

2. Do you have to repay an overpayment?

You can be asked to pay back any overpayment, even if it was caused by a Department for Work and Pensions (DWP) mistake. This means that you cannot appeal against a decision to recover

Coronavirus

During the coronavirus pandemic, the DWP temporarily suspended recovery of overpayments, including overpayments of universal credit. This suspension lasted until July 2020.

an overpayment. However, if you believe that you were not overpaid at all, or that the amount of the overpayment is wrong, you can appeal about this. Before you can appeal, you must ask the DWP to reconsider its decision. The DWP does not stop recovering the overpayment while this is being decided.

Although you cannot appeal about recovery, you can ask the DWP to make the repayments more manageable – eg, by allowing you to

---

EXAMPLE

Overpayments

Dot gets a childcare costs element in her universal credit to help pay for her daughter's after-school club. The DWP tells her she has been paid too much universal credit and revises her award. She is told she owes £400 and repayments start being deducted from her monthly payments. Dot is now short of money and does the following.

- She asks in her universal credit online journal for an explanation. She is told that universal credit was still paying for a breakfast club that her daughter used to attend, as well as the after-school club.

- She checks whether the amount of the overpayment is correct. She discovers that it is too high. The childcare costs included are still wrong. She asks the DWP to reconsider the amount of the overpayment. She plans to appeal if it is not corrected.

- She asks the DWP to write off the overpayment. She explains how it was the DWP's fault, not hers. She also explains that she has an anxiety condition which has got much worse because she fears losing her job as a direct result of paying back the overpayment. She says she cannot afford to pay her bills as well as pay for travel to work and childcare costs.

- She gets advice from a local advice centre. An adviser helps with her appeal about the amount of the overpayment and helps make her case to have the overpayment written off.

pay back at a lower rate. You can also ask that some, or all, of the overpayment be written off. The DWP has guidance that says it will consider these options if paying back the money:

- would mean financial hardship for you – you are asked for details of your regular income and spending
- could affect your health, or the health of someone in your family – you may be asked for medical evidence
- could cause particular upset in the family – you should explain the circumstances

The guidance does not say that an overpayment will be written off just because it was the DWP's mistake. You could still ask for this, but you should also explain the effect on your family if you would have to repay the overpayment.

What CPAG says

Overpayments

- Check your award carefully. If you disagree that you have been overpaid or with the amount you have been overpaid, ask for this to be reconsidered and then appeal if the DWP does not revise it.

- If paying back the overpayment will cause you hardship or affect your family's health or welfare, ask for some or all of it to be written off.

- If the DWP does not do as you ask, consider using its internal complaints procedure.

- If you are still unhappy, you can take your case to the Independent Case Examiner.

- Contact your MP and ask for her/his help – eg, by taking the complaint to the Parliamentary and Health Service Ombudsman.

- In exceptional cases, you might be able to make a legal challenge, called a 'judicial review'. Get advice about this.

3. How do you repay an overpayment?

The Department for Work and Pensions (DWP) can recover an overpayment of universal credit by:

- making deductions from an ongoing award of benefit you have
- reducing an amount of arrears of benefit that is owed to you
- making deductions from your earnings
- taking court action against you

The usual way of repaying an overpayment is from your ongoing award of benefit. This might be universal credit or it might be another benefit. Deductions can be made from most benefits, but not from child benefit or guardian's allowance. The maximum amount that can be deducted from your universal credit for an overpayment is normally 15 per cent of your 'standard allowance'. However, it can be more than this if you have earnings, if fraud is involved or if 'hardship payments' are being recovered.

If you are employed, the DWP can recover an overpayment of universal credit from your earnings. The DWP sends a notice to you and your employer, telling you both how much will be deducted.

What CPAG says

Repaying an overpayment

Ask for lower repayments if they are causing you hardship, or affecting your health or welfare, or your family's health or welfare. Explain how your difficulties are caused by repaying the money.

You might have other deductions from your universal credit at the same time – eg, for rent arrears or to repay a tax credit overpayment. In practice, the total amount taken off your universal credit cannot usually be more than 30 per cent of your 'standard allowance' unless you have rent arrears or a fuel debt and deducting more is considered to be in your best interests. You can also ask for these other deductions to be reduced.

The DWP has the discretion to reduce other deductions being made from your universal credit. If you are told that the creditor must decide, insist that the DWP considers your request.

No deduction is made if your net earnings are less than £100 a week or £430 a month (in 2020/21), unless the overpayment is connected to a benefit offence for which you have been found guilty. Your employer can also deduct up to a £1 administration charge from your earnings each time it makes a deduction for an overpayment.

The DWP can recover an overpayment of universal credit through the courts. It might do so if it cannot recover in another way – eg, if you are not receiving any benefits and are not working. Court costs can be added to and treated as part of the overpayment. There are time limits in which the DWP must start court action. There is no time limit for recovering overpayments in other ways.

EXAMPLES

Repaying an overpayment

Mona has been getting universal credit as someone with limited capability for work but starts a part-time job. Her award is adjusted. A year later, the DWP decides it has miscalculated her entitlement since she started working. Her award is revised and the amount she has been overpaid is worked out. The DWP decides to recover the overpayment and to do so from both her ongoing universal credit award and her earnings, as her current award is low and the rate of recovery from her earnings will not cause her hardship. Her employer makes the deductions the DWP has requested from Mona's wages.

Saleem is having money deducted from his universal credit to repay an advance payment, a tax credit debt and a universal credit overpayment. The DWP is deducting the maximum 30 per cent from his usual monthly payment of £409.89. He is left with £286.92 a month. Saleem asks for lower repayments and provides details of his income and expenses that show financial hardship. His request is accepted and his monthly universal credit payment increases to £307.41.

Further information

The DWP's *Benefit Overpayment Recovery Guide*, containing guidance for staff to follow when deciding how and when to recover an overpayment, is available at gov.uk/government/publications/benefit-overpayment-recovery-staff-guide.

Chapter 9
Challenging a decision

This chapter covers:

1. Do you disagree with a decision?

2. How do you complain?

What you need to know

- If you are unhappy with a decision about your universal credit, you can usually appeal to an independent tribunal. Before you do so, you must ask the Department for Work and Pensions to look at the decision again.

- Even if you cannot appeal, you can still complain about the way your universal credit claim has been handled.

1. Do you disagree with a decision?

You can challenge a decision about your universal credit with which you do not agree.

First, you should ask the Department for Work and Pensions (DWP) to look at its decision again. This is called asking for a 'mandatory reconsideration'. The DWP can look at the decision again if you request this within a month of the date the decision was sent to you. If it has been longer than a month, a decision can still be looked at again if there are special reasons to extend the time limit and you make your request within 13 months of the decision. As long as you ask for the decision to be looked at again within this time limit, you will be able to appeal if you remain unhappy with the decision. If the decision was sent to you more than 13 months ago, you can still ask for it to be looked at again, but you cannot appeal.

Box A
Requesting a mandatory reconsideration

You can ask for a mandatory reconsideration:

- over the phone
- in person at the job centre
- in writing – you can print a mandatory reconsideration request form via gov.uk/government/publications/challenge-a-decision-made-by-the-department-for-work-and-pensions-dwp
- by putting a note in your online journal

Mandatory reconsiderations requested via online journals are not always processed. If you do not hear from the DWP about your request, check whether it has been received. Although you can just say that you want the decision to be looked at again, to avoid confusion it is best to say that you want a mandatory reconsideration.

Once the DWP makes a decision, it should send you a 'mandatory reconsideration notice' explaining your right to appeal if you are still not happy. You can appeal against most decisions, but not about whether to recover an overpayment or what your 'work-related requirements' are. Once you have this notice, you can then appeal to an independent appeal tribunal.

There are strict time limits for appealing. You should appeal within one month of being sent the mandatory reconsideration notice, although the time limits can be extended for special reasons. You should appeal by completing Form SSCS1, which is available from gov.uk/government/publications/appeal-a-social-security-benefits-decision-form-sscs1.

EXAMPLE

Disagreeing with a decision

Ilona gets universal credit for herself and her child. She has mental health problems and has been getting an additional element in her award because she is ill. At her next medical examination, she is assessed as being fit for work. She receives a decision saying that her universal credit award will no longer include the additional element. Ilona believes she is too ill to work and wants to challenge this. She is not sure how to do so and contacts the DWP to say she wants to appeal. Because the rules say she must first ask for a mandatory reconsideration, the DWP treats this as a request for a mandatory reconsideration. The DWP reconsiders the decision and decides not to make any revisions. Ilona can now appeal. She makes her written appeal immediately so she does not miss the deadline, and goes to her local advice centre for help to make her case.

2. How do you complain?

If you disagree with a decision on your universal credit award or payment, first check whether you can ask for this to be changed by using the 'mandatory reconsideration' and appeal process.

If you are unhappy with the way your universal credit claim has been handled, you can make a complaint. For instance, you may want to complain about:

- a delay in dealing with your claim
- poor administration in the benefit office
- poor advice from the Department for Work and Pensions (DWP)
- poor administration or advice from staff helping you look for, or prepare for, work
- a poorly conducted medical examination
- the way the system affects you

If you are unhappy with the way your claim has been handled by the DWP, you should first take this up with the office dealing with your claim. Contact details should be on any letters you have about your claim. You may find it helpful to speak to the manager of your local job centre. If this does not resolve the issue, the DWP has a complaints procedure (for universal credit this procedure includes being able to make the complaint online). This can be found at gov.uk/government/organisations/department-for-work-pensions/about/complaints-procedure.

If you are unhappy with the service, advice or administration from a provider contracted by the DWP to carry out employment support services, you should first contact the provider and use its complaints procedure.

Medical examinations are conducted by the Health Assessment Advisory Service (Maximus). To complain about the conduct of a medical examination or about the healthcare professional who carried it out, contact the provider and use its complaints procedure.

Once you have gone through all the steps in the complaints procedure, if you are still unhappy with the response, you can take your case to the Independent Case Examiner. This deals with complaints about the DWP and its contracted providers. It can settle complaints by agreement between you and the DWP or provider, or carry out an investigation and make recommendations about how a complaint should be settled. If you are still not happy, you can contact your MP and ask her/him to refer your complaint to the Parliamentary and Health Service Ombudsman.

How do you use your MP?

If you do not have a particular universal credit issue to resolve, but you are unhappy with the way the system affects you, you may wish to take this up with your local MP.

You can also take up a specific problem with your MP. Usually it is best to do this if you have already tried to resolve the problem directly with the Department for Work and Pensions but are still dissatisfied. In particular, it can be useful to ask your MP for help if there has been a delay in your claim being dealt with.

You can email or write to your MP, or go to a local 'surgery' – ie, the regular sessions that MPs usually have to meet their constituents.

Further information

For information and tactical tips on appeals, see CPAG's guide *Winning Your Benefit Appeal: what you need to know.*
To find out who your MP is and how to contact her/him, see parliament.uk. You can also find contact details in your local library or town hall, or you can write to your local MP at the House of Commons, London SW1A 0AA.

Customer Relations Team
Health Assessment Advisory Service (Maximus)
Room 4E04
Quarry House,
Quarry Hill
Leeds LS2 7UA
Tel: 0800 288 8777
email: customer-relations@chdauk.co.uk
chdauk.co.uk

Independent Case Examiner
PO Box 209
Bootle L20 7WA
Tel: 0800 414 8529
NGT text relay: 18001 then 0800 414 8529
email: ice@dwp.gov.uk
gov.uk/government/organisations/independent-case-examiner

Parliamentary and Health Service Ombudsman
Millbank Tower
30 Millbank
London SW1P 4QP
Tel: 0345 015 4033
ombudsman.org.uk

Chapter 10
Universal credit and specific groups of people

This chapter covers:

1. Lone parents

2. Families with three or more children

3. Carers

4. Disabled people

5. Young people

6. Older people

7. People from abroad

What you need to know

- Almost anyone of working age can claim, provided they meet the basic rules of entitlement and the financial conditions.

- Your personal or family circumstances determine how much universal credit you get and what 'work-related requirements' you must meet.

- There are special rules that allow some 16/17 year olds and some young people in education to claim universal credit.

- People over pension age cannot usually get universal credit.

- Certain people from abroad are excluded from universal credit.

1. Lone parents

Can lone parents claim universal credit?

Lone parents can claim universal credit.

You are a lone parent if you are responsible for a child who normally lives with you and you do not have a partner living with you.

If you are a lone parent, you make a single claim for universal credit. It is important to be clear about whether you are a lone parent and be aware that if a partner moves in with you, even if s/he is not your child's parent, you become a couple and must make a joint claim for universal credit.

Are there any special rules?

If you are a lone parent, the maximum amount of universal credit payable to you is based on an allowance for yourself and your child(ren), plus an amount for some housing costs and, if you are in work, an amount for your childcare costs. There are additional amounts if you care for a disabled child or adult, or if you or your child are ill or disabled. There is no additional amount specifically for lone parents.

If you are working, because you have a child you can earn a certain amount before the amount of your universal credit is affected (called a 'work allowance'). There is more information on how universal credit is calculated in Chapter 5.

If you share the care of your children with a former partner, it is not possible to split payments for children. You can agree who should claim for your child or, if you cannot agree, the Department for Work and Pensions decides which one of you has the main responsibility. This does not automatically go to whoever claimed universal credit first, or who gets child benefit, but takes into account a range of factors. If it is decided that you do not have main responsibility for a child, you are not treated as a lone parent. This means you are not entitled to additional amounts for the child and you must meet the 'work-related requirements' that apply to your other circumstances. The amount you can get to help with your rent may also be reduced if you have a spare bedroom for your child to stay with you. Chapter 5 explains about this 'bedroom tax'.

What are your work-related requirements?
Your 'work-related requirements' depend on the age of your youngest child.

Box A
The work-related requirements for lone parents

- If you have a child under the age of one, you have no work-related requirements.

- If you have a child aged one, you must attend 'work-focused interviews', usually every six months.

- If you have a child aged two, you must attend 'work-focused interviews' and prepare for work. This involves undertaking activity that makes it more likely that you will return to work in the future.

- Once your youngest child turns three, you must search for work and be available to take up a job. You are allowed to place some restrictions on the type of work and the hours you are prepared to do. If your child has not yet started school, you can usually limit your expected hours of work to 16 a week and perhaps fewer, depending on whether a suitable childcare place is available.

- As long as you have a child aged under 13, you can limit your expected hours of work to fit in with your child's usual school or nursery hours, including travel, so you only need to be available for work while s/he is at school or nursery. This will usually be for 25 hours a week but may be fewer if school hours are reduced during the coronavirus pandemic.

- Most people are required to attend an interview or take up a job immediately. As a lone parent, you may be allowed up to one month's notice to take up work or 48 hours' notice to attend an interview, taking into account how long you need to arrange childcare.

You may have fewer work-related requirements if you have experienced domestic violence, or if your partner or child has died within the previous six months. Your requirements may also be relaxed in other temporary circumstances or if your usual childcare arrangements are disrupted.

EXAMPLE

Work-related requirements

Martha is a lone parent with one child aged six. She gets universal credit and must search for work and be available for work. Her claimant commitment allows her to restrict her availability to school hours during term time only. She is asked to attend a skills assessment course for two weeks while her child is at school. If she refuses to go, she is likely to be given a sanction and the amount of her universal credit reduced. She is offered a temporary job of four hours a day during school hours, three days a week. If she does not accept the job, she may receive a sanction. The job continues to be available during the school holidays. Martha can get help with 85 per cent of her childcare costs in her universal credit, so she can continue working. If suitable childcare is not available, she should not get a sanction for giving up the job.

Do you have childcare costs?

Universal credit can include an amount to help with your childcare costs (a 'childcare costs element') if you are working and paying a registered childcare provider, such as a childminder, nursery or after-school club.

There is no minimum number of hours you must work to qualify for help with childcare – any work can qualify, provided the amount of childcare is not considered excessive in relation to how many hours you work.

The full costs of your childcare are not covered – only 85 per cent of the costs are covered, up to a maximum amount of £646 a month for one child or £1,108 for two or more children.

Universal credit can cover childcare costs that you incur before starting work if you have been offered a job that is due to start in the following universal credit 'assessment period', to allow a settling-in period for your child.

If you pay for childcare costs in advance, the childcare must be provided in either of the next two assessment periods. The amount paid in advance is included in the assessment period in which the childcare is provided.

Universal credit cannot include an amount that is paid or reimbursed by someone else (eg, your employer) or covered by other support.

You can continue to have your childcare costs included in your universal credit for one assessment period after stopping work, to allow you to find another job without losing the childcare place.

You must report your actual childcare costs in the assessment period in which you paid them, or the following assessment period. If you report them late, they are only included in your universal credit if you have a good reason. It is your responsibility to report your childcare costs, not the childcare provider's, although your provider may be required to confirm the costs. There is no system of automatic notification as there is with earnings. You are usually asked to provide evidence of the amount you have paid in each monthly assessment period.

Are there other benefits for lone parents?

- **Child benefit** remains outside the universal credit system and is administered by HM Revenue and Customs. You should claim child benefit for your child(ren), as well as universal credit. There is no limit on how many children you can get child benefit for. You do not have to claim child benefit to prove that you are responsible for a child for universal credit (but it may help to do so).

- Lone parents who have been bereaved can claim **bereavement support payment**. Bereavement support payment is not taken into account as income when your universal credit is assessed.

- In England and Wales, you can get a **Sure Start maternity grant** if you get universal credit. This is £500 to help with the costs of a new baby, but it is usually only payable for your first child. It does not matter about other income or whether you are in work, provided you are entitled to universal credit.

- In Scotland, you can get a **Best Start grant** if you get universal credit. For a new baby, this is £600 for your first child or £300 if you have another child younger than 16 living with you. An early learning payment of £250 when your child is aged from two to three and a half, and a school-age payment of £250 when your child is able to start school (from 1 June in the calendar year in which s/he turns five; unless born in January/February, in which case it is the calendar year in which s/he turns four, to the end of February the following year).

- If you are pregnant or have a child under four years old, you get universal credit and your take-home pay is £408 or less a month, you qualify for **Healthy Start vouchers** for milk, vegetables, fruit and free vitamins. Telephone the Healthy Start helpline on 0345 607 6823 for more information. In Scotland, you can get the **Best Start foods payment card** if you are pregnant or if you have a child under three years old, you get universal credit and your take-home pay is £610 or less a month.

2. Families with three or more children

Can families with three or more children claim universal credit?

You can claim universal credit if you have three or more children, but you may not be able to get a 'child element' included for a third or subsequent child born on or after 6 April 2017. That is known as the 'two-child limit'.

You can get a child element for all children born before 6 April 2017. You may be able to get a child element for a third or subsequent child born on or after 6 April 2017 if an exception applies. The order of children (ie, whether a child is your first, second or third child) is decided by their date of birth, with the earliest first.

What CPAG says

Families with three or more children

If you have three or more children, you may be affected by the two-child limit. This was introduced from April 2017 with the government intention that families should think carefully about whether they are financially prepared to support a new child without relying on means-tested benefits. However, even if you were financially able to support three or more children when you had them, the policy will still affect you if your third or subsequent child was born on or after 6 April 2017.

Are there any special rules?

Even if you cannot have a 'child element' included in your universal credit award for a third or subsequent child, you can still have an additional amount included for that child if s/he is disabled. You can also get help with your childcare costs for that child. There are also exceptions to this 'two-child limit'.

Box B
Exceptions to the two-child limit

- **Multiple births.** This exception recognises that families do not plan to have a multiple birth. If a child is born in a multiple birth and you already have two or more children in your household, you get a child element for all but one of the children. If you have one child and then have a multiple birth, you get a child element for all the children. If you have no other children and have a multiple birth, you get a child element for all the children.

- **Adopted children.** If you adopt a child in the UK, an exception applies to that child. You get a child element for her/him and s/he is not counted for the purposes of the two-child limit, so you can also get a child element for two other children.

(continued)

(Box B continued)

- **Friend and family carers.** If you look after a child under a formal caring arrangement or informally and the child would otherwise be 'looked after' by a local authority, an exception applies to that child. You get a child element for her/him, and s/he is not counted for the purposes of the two-child limit, so you can also get a child element for two other children. You must provide evidence of the legal arrangement or a form completed by a social worker.

- **Under 16 year olds who have a child.** If a young person under 16 in your household becomes a parent and you are responsible for the new child who is a third or subsequent child in your household, an exception applies to that child, and s/he is not counted as part of the two-child limit.

- **Non-consensual conception.** If you have a third or subsequent child who is likely to have been conceived as a result of rape or in a 'controlling or coercive relationship', an exception applies to that child. You must not be living at the same address as the alleged perpetrator and you must provide evidence of a criminal conviction or criminal injuries compensation award, or a form completed by a health professional, social worker or other approved person.

EXAMPLE

The two-child limit

Penny is in receipt of universal credit and has two children. She gives birth to twins on 30 June 2020. A child element is not paid for the first twin, but an exception applies to the other twin. Penny's universal credit award includes three child elements in total.

> **EXAMPLE**
>
> **The two-child limit**
>
> Mark and Mary get universal credit. They have one child of their own born in 2012, Jack. They became legal guardians for Mary's niece, Bethan, in May 2015, after Mary's sister died. In July 2020, Mary gives birth to another child, Harry. Because they are legal guardians for Bethan, she is not counted for the purposes of the two-child limit. Mark and Mary have three child elements included in their universal credit award.

3. Carers

Can carers claim universal credit?

Carers can claim universal credit.

You can get a 'carer element' included in your universal credit if you care for a severely disabled person and you are not paid to provide care. To be recognised as severely disabled, the person you look after must get the middle or highest rate of the disability living allowance 'care component', either rate of the 'daily living component' of personal independence payment or either rate of attendance allowance. You can get a carer element even though you do not get carer's allowance.

Are there any special rules?

There is an additional amount in universal credit (a 'carer element') for people who have 'regular and substantial' caring responsibilities for a severely disabled person. This means that you provide care for at least 35 hours a week.

You can get the carer element whether or not you have made a claim for carer's allowance. If you have claimed carer's allowance and you meet the conditions, but have been told that it cannot be paid because you get another benefit (such as contributory employment and support allowance), you can still be treated as a carer for universal credit. If you cannot claim carer's allowance because you earn over the earnings limit, but you meet the other conditions, you can still be treated as a carer for universal credit, even if you have not actually claimed carer's allowance.

Before applying, bear in mind that getting a carer element could mean that the person you care for gets less benefit. This is because the 'severe disability premium' that is sometimes paid in other benefits (eg, pension credit and employment and support allowance) stops.

If more than one person is caring for the same disabled person, the carer element can only be paid to one of you. If you are in a couple and you are both carers, you can get two carer elements, but you must be looking after different people. If you both look after the same person, you should decide who is the main carer, otherwise the Department for Work and Pensions (DWP) decides for you, and the other partner usually has to look for work.

EXAMPLE

Carers

Sue and Richard care for their daughter who gets the middle rate care component of disability living allowance. Sue works and Richard has limited capability for work-related activity. Although both Sue and Richard are carers, they nominate Sue as the main carer. Their work coach is satisfied that she spends at least 35 hours a week looking after their daughter, which she fits in around her working hours. Their universal credit award includes the carer element for Sue and the limited capability for work-related activity element for Richard.

If they had nominated Richard as the main carer, their award would only have included the limited capability for work-related activity element, as the two elements cannot be awarded in respect of the same person.

If you are also disabled, you cannot get the carer element at the same time as the additional amount paid because of your disability (a 'limited capability for work' or 'limited capability for work-related activity' element). If you are a disabled carer, make this clear on your claim – the DWP must award the element of the highest value. If you are in a couple, you can get a carer element for yourself and a limited capability for work or limited capability for work-related activity element for your disabled partner.

If you are in work, your earnings affect the amount of universal credit you get, in the same way as other claimants. There is no 'work allowance' for carers. However, you do not lose the carer element just because you are working (even if you earn more than the limit for carer's allowance – £128 in 2020/21), provided you are still caring for at least 35 hours a week.

What CPAG says

Carers not getting carer's allowance

If you are not getting carer's allowance, the DWP may not accept that you are a carer. There is no set way of assessing and deciding that you are a carer for universal credit, and no definition of what counts as caring for someone, although it can include the preparation involved for providing care, and clearing up afterwards. If you have declared that you are a carer but have not been awarded the carer element, request a 'mandatory reconsideration' and appeal if necessary. If this continues to be an ongoing problem, you could consider claiming carer's allowance, so that your carer status is recognised by a different section of the DWP. The person you care for must sign the carer's allowance application form to confirm you are her/his carer. Get advice about the potential impact on the disabled person's benefits before you claim carer's allowance or the carer element.

> ## Box C
> ## Foster carers
>
> - Foster carers who are legally approved to look after a child or young person by arrangement with a local authority or voluntary organisation are treated differently from carers looking after a disabled person.
>
> - There are special rules for foster carers in universal credit.
>
> - In Scotland, kinship carers of looked after children are treated in the same way as foster carers.
>
> - Lone foster carers are only required to attend 'work-focused interviews'. They do not have any other 'work-related requirements' until their youngest foster child reaches 16 years old, when they are required to look for, and be available for, work.
>
> - In exceptional circumstances, when a foster child who is 16 or 17 needs full-time care, the foster carer is only required to participate in work-focused interviews and has no other work-related requirements, until the child reaches 18 or the placement ends.
>
> - Fostering couples must say which one of them is the lead carer. The lead carer is only required to attend work-focused interviews and has no other work-related requirements. The other member of the couple has all the work-related requirements that apply in her/his circumstances, unless there are exceptional circumstances and the foster child needs full-time care by two adults.
>
> - Fostering is not treated as being self-employed or in work.
>
> - Fostering payments are not taken into account as earnings or income. There is no additional amount in universal credit for being a foster carer.

What are your work-related requirements?

Carers who spend at least 35 hours a week caring for a severely disabled person do not have any 'work-related requirements', so you can get universal credit without being expected to look for work.

If you do not qualify for a 'carer element', you may also have no work-related requirements in the following circumstances.

- You care for more than one severely disabled person and your total caring responsibilities amount to at least 35 hours a week.

- You care for a severely disabled person for at least 35 hours a week, but you are not the main carer – eg, because someone else gets a carer element for looking after her/him.

In these two situations, the DWP must be satisfied that it is unreasonable to expect you to look for work, even within agreed limits.

Otherwise, if you do not get the carer element in your universal credit award (eg, you spend less than 35 hours a week caring, or the person you care for does not get the middle or highest rate of the disability living allowance 'care component', either rate of the 'daily living component' of personal independence payment or either rate of attendance allowance), you are expected to look for work, within limits if agreed in your 'claimant commitment'. You can restrict the hours you are available for, and searching for, work to be compatible with your caring responsibilities, provided this is agreed and you still have a reasonable chance of finding work.

This may also apply if the disabled person is waiting to hear about a new claim for personal independence payment, attendance allowance or disability living allowance. However, you are not automatically treated as a carer while her/his claim is being decided, so any flexibility in your work-related requirements must be agreed in your claimant commitment.

EXAMPLE

Carers

Duncan looks after his brother, who gets the daily living component of personal independence payment. Duncan gets universal credit and has no work-related requirements. His brother's personal independence payment stops following a review. Duncan no longer meets the conditions for being a carer for a severely disabled person, so must now meet all the work-related requirements. His work coach is satisfied that his brother still has a disability and so he is able to agree some restrictions in his claimant commitment on his hours of availability for work and the notice required to attend an interview or take up a job. Duncan must still show that he is taking all reasonable action to find work within the agreed restrictions, otherwise he may be given a sanction and the amount of his universal credit may be reduced.

What CPAG says

Waiting to hear about the disabled person's benefit claim

You are not treated as a carer for the work-related requirements while you are waiting for the disabled person's claim for a disability benefit to be decided. If you are in this situation, explain your caring responsibilities to your 'work coach', so that your work-related requirements can be adjusted. If you fail to meet a work-related requirement because of your caring responsibilities, you should explain this. You should not be given a 'sanction' if you had a good reason.

Are there other benefits for carers?

Carers can claim **carer's allowance**. You must spend at least 35 hours a week looking after a severely disabled person who gets the middle or highest rate of disability living allowance 'care component', either rate of the 'daily living component' of personal independence payment, or either rate of attendance allowance. You cannot get carer's allowance if you are a full-time student or if you earn more than £128 a week (in 2020/21). During the coronavirus pandemic, you can continue to qualify for carer's allowance if you are unable to provide care because you or the person you look after is in isolation or is infected by coronavirus.

Carer's allowance counts in full as income for universal credit. However, as it is not enough to live on, you may get a top-up of universal credit as well.

In Scotland, if you get carer's allowance, you can also get a carer's allowance supplement. If you are aged 16 to 18 and don't get carer's allowance, you may be able to get a young carer grant from Social Security Scotland. Carer's allowance will be replaced by a Scottish equivalent in future.

4. Disabled people

Can disabled people claim universal credit?

People with disabilities can claim universal credit. However, if you are currently getting an old 'means-tested benefit' that includes a 'severe disability premium', you cannot currently claim universal credit. At some point, the Department for Work and Pensions (DWP) will transfer your claim to universal credit. There is more information about this in Chapter 2.

You may be entitled to an extra amount in your universal credit if you are disabled. There are different rules for adults and children.

What CPAG says

Claiming online

The process of claiming universal credit online can be a significant barrier to some disabled people. If you cannot claim online because of your disability, official guidance says that a home visit can be arranged by the DWP or, in exceptional cases, the details for your claim can be taken by telephone. However, in practice, this is often difficult – you or your adviser or advocate must be persistent and explain your difficulties in detail in order to get the DWP to agree. If you need a British Sign Language interpreter at an interview, this must be arranged.

Are there any special rules?

There are special rules for some people with a disability. These affect how much universal credit you get, what kind of 'work-related requirements' you have and, if you work, how much you can earn before your universal credit is affected.

Universal credit includes additional amounts for adults who are unable to work or undertake work-related activity, and for disabled children, paid at one of two rates, depending on the severity of the disability.

The additional amount you get for a disabled child depends on the amount of disability living allowance or personal independence payment s/he gets. The additional amount you get for a disabled adult (a 'limited capability for work element' or 'limited capability for work-related activity element') depends on a medical assessment of your capability for work.

Note: you cannot get the limited capability for work element if your period of limited capability for work started on or after 3 April 2017. However, it is still possible to be assessed as having limited capability for work and this is worthwhile – it means you can keep more of your earnings before your universal credit is affected (a 'work allowance') and your work-related requirements are less (you only need to prepare for work, rather than look for work).

What CPAG says

Waiting for a medical assessment

If you have claimed universal credit and are waiting for a medical assessment, it should be carried out within three months but may take longer. You have all the work-related requirements while you are waiting to be assessed. However, your 'work coach' has the discretion to relax these during this period, so make sure you provide more details and evidence of your disability or health condition.

If your income is too high to qualify for universal credit unless you are awarded the limited capability for work-related activity element, you should be awarded a token amount of one penny until the assessment is carried out.

If you are a full-time student and will only be entitled to universal credit after you have been assessed as having limited capability for work (you must also be entitled to personal independence payment), you must also claim contributory employment and support allowance to ensure your assessment is carried out.

During the coronavirus pandemic, face-to-face assessments are suspended, but can be carried out by telephone or based on paper evidence.

If you are disabled and you also care for someone who is disabled, you cannot get an additional amount for your disability as well as a 'carer element' in your universal credit. However, if you are in a couple and you are disabled and your partner is a carer, you can get a limited capability for work or a limited capability for work-related activity element for yourself and a carer element for your partner.

There is more on the additional amounts in Chapter 5.

What CPAG says

Are you worse off on universal credit?

Many disabled people are worse off on universal credit than they were on the old 'means-tested benefits'. This is because universal credit has no additional amounts for adults equivalent to the old disability premiums, which were based on receipt of a disability benefit, and amounts for some disabled children are lower than the equivalent in child tax credit. The 'transitional SDP amount' for claimants who were entitled to a 'severe disability premium' and the rule preventing new universal credit claims in this situation have addressed the problem for some severely disabled people who lost (or stood to lose) a lot when moving on to universal credit. However, it does not mean that all disabled people are protected. You may still lose out if you claim universal credit before you are notified to do so under 'managed migration', so it is important to get independent advice before claiming.

Are you working?

Disabled people can earn more than some other claimants before their universal credit is reduced. This is called a 'work allowance'. You qualify for this disregard if you or your partner have been assessed as having 'limited capability for work' or 'limited capability for work-related activity'.

If you have been assessed as having limited capability for work and you start working, you are not automatically treated as no longer having limited capability for work or work-related activity, so you do not necessarily lose the additional amount in your universal credit award and your work allowance. However, your capability for work may be reassessed.

If you become disabled while you are in work and your monthly earnings are at least 16 times the national minimum wage a week, you can only be newly assessed as having limited capability for work and work-related activity (in order to get the work allowance and an additional amount in your universal credit), if you already get disability living allowance or personal independence payment.

> **EXAMPLE**
>
> **Disabled person**
>
> Sarah is a single person who has previously been in good health, working 20 hours a week on the minimum wage. She gets universal credit, but is expected to look for better paid work or more hours. She is diagnosed with a long-term health condition and believes that this is affecting her ability to work. She does not want to give up her job, but feels that she should be entitled to additional support through universal credit as a disabled worker. She asks to be assessed for limited capability for work, which would allow more of her earnings to be ignored, and she would not have to look for more work. Her request is refused because she is already working more than 16 hours a week. She must therefore first apply for personal independence payment. If this is awarded, she can then be assessed as having limited capability for work for universal credit.

Are there other benefits for disabled people?

You can claim **contributory employment and support allowance** if you are unable to work, and have worked in the past and paid enough national insurance contributions. Payment is limited to one year unless you are assessed as having 'limited capability for work-related activity', in which case it can be paid indefinitely. You can get contributory employment and support allowance at the same time as universal credit, but it counts in full as income, so reduces your entitlement. In some situations, you can get contributory employment and support allowance if you cannot get universal credit – eg, if your savings are too high. If you are entitled to contributory employment and support allowance and universal credit, or you move from one to another, the rules on 'work-related requirements', 'sanctions' and 'hardship payments' apply to both benefits.

You can claim **personal independence payment** if you have a disability that affects your mobility or ability to carry out daily living activities. If your child (aged under 16) is disabled, you can claim **disability living allowance** for her/him. You can continue to receive disability living allowance or personal independence payment in addition to your universal credit, as these remain outside the universal credit system. They do not count as income. These will be replaced by Scottish equivalent benefits in future.

5. Young people

Can young people claim universal credit?

In general, you must be at least 18 years old to claim universal credit. However, there are special rules that allow some young people aged 16 and 17 to claim.

If you are under 16, you cannot claim universal credit in any circumstance. A responsible adult with whom you live should claim for you, or the local authority must have responsibility for you.

Are there any special rules?

If you are aged 16 or 17, you can claim universal credit for yourself, any housing costs you are liable for and any children you are responsible for if:

- you have a child or are about to have a baby
- you are 'without parental support'
- you are disabled or ill
- you are a carer

Chapter 3 explains more about when you can claim in these situations.

If you are a care leaver aged 16 or 17, you cannot usually get universal credit and the local authority still has a duty to support you. You can only get universal credit as a care leaver if you are disabled or responsible for a child.

If you are 18 or over, there are no special rules. However, if you are still in education, you may be classed as a student and so cannot get universal credit. There are exceptions, such as if you are in non-advanced education and 'without parental support'. More information about studying is in Chapter 3.

EXAMPLE

Young person estranged from parents

Zoe is aged 17 and has recently left school and started work. She has an argument with her parents and leaves home. She finds a room in private rented accommodation, and claims universal credit. She is below the normal qualifying age of 18, and must make a statement explaining that she is estranged from her parents. The Department for Work and Pensions looks at her statement and its own guidance, which says there is no requirement to corroborate such evidence or contact parents. Zoe should be believed, unless her statement is self-contradictory or improbable.

If you are under 25, you get less universal credit than people aged 25 and over, including if you are responsible for a child or if you are disabled. If you are aged 18 to 21, you may have to take part in a 'youth obligation support' programme, with more 'work-related requirements', including applying for an apprenticeship, traineeship, work experience or work placement.

Are there other benefits for young people?

There are not many other benefits that young people aged 16 or 17 can claim for themselves. If you are disabled, you may be able to claim **personal independence payment**. If you are a carer, you may be able to claim **carer's allowance**, or in Scotland, a **young carer grant**. You can only claim 'contributory benefits', such as contribution-based jobseeker's allowance or contributory employment and support allowance, if you have worked and paid enough national insurance contributions, usually for two to three years before you claim.

6. Older people

Can older people claim universal credit?

Older people under pension age can claim universal credit. Pension age is 66 from 6 October 2020. People older than pension age cannot usually get universal credit and can claim pension credit instead. If you are single, you cannot stay on universal credit when you reach pension age – your universal credit ends. Your award is terminated, either from the start of the assessment period, or from the day you turn pension age if you claimed pension credit in advance. From November 2020, this rule will change so that you will receive a universal credit payment for the whole assessment period in which you turn pension age. Before then, the government has said it will make equivalent payments on an extra-statutory basis so you should not lose out if you haven't claimed pension credit in advance. If you are in a couple, when one of you reaches pension age your universal credit can continue until you both reach pension age (but retirement pension counts in full as your income).

You cannot usually make a new claim for pension credit if your partner is under pension age. However, if you were already getting pension credit as a couple before 15 May 2019, you can stay on it, even though one of you is under pension age. If one of you reached pension age before 15 May 2019, you can still make a new claim for pension credit if you have been entitled to housing benefit in the same couple since before 15 May 2019 (and you are not on income support, income-based jobseeker's allowance, income-related employment and support allowance or universal credit). In these situations, you can stay on pension credit once you are entitled to it, and you do not have to claim universal credit.

If you claim universal credit by mistake and are entitled to it, your pension credit ends and you cannot claim it again until you have both reached pension age. If you are getting pension credit as a single person, and a partner under pension age moves in with you, your pension credit (and housing benefit if you are getting it) ends and you must claim universal credit as a couple.

You cannot get both pension credit and universal credit at the same time, and you cannot make separate claims if you are a couple.

Are there any special rules?

There is no additional amount for older people in universal credit.

If you are claiming universal credit as a couple, only the working-age partner has 'work-related requirements'. However, if s/he fails to meet her/his requirements, you are given a sanction as a couple and the amount of your universal credit is reduced for a period of time.

If the partner older than pension age is getting attendance allowance, or the enhanced rate of the daily living component of personal independence payment, or highest rate of the care component of disability living allowance, s/he is treated as having limited capability for work-related activity, which means an additional element can be included in the universal credit award. If s/he is getting personal independence payment or disability living allowance at any other rate or component, s/he is treated as having limited capability for work, which means a work allowance is included, so that you can earn up to a certain level before universal credit is reduced.

Are there other benefits for older people

Universal credit does not replace **pension credit**. You cannot get pension credit and universal credit at the same time, except for in the assessment period in which you turn pension age, when pension credit can start from pension age, and a payment of universal credit is made for the whole of that assessment period. Pension credit includes additional amounts for children, replacing child tax credit. From October 2023, it is intended that pension credit will also include amounts for rent, replacing housing benefit. Both members of a couple must have reached pension age to make a new claim.

Universal credit does not replace **retirement pensions**. If you get a retirement pension and your partner is under pension age, you can get universal credit, but your pension is counted in full as income.

Attendance allowance and the **winter fuel payment** remain outside the universal credit system and are not counted as income when working out how much universal credit you get.

7. People from abroad

Can people from abroad claim universal credit?

You can only get universal credit if you meet the immigration and residence conditions.

The immigration conditions apply to people who are not British citizens.

You meet these conditions for universal credit if, for example, you are a European national with settled status, or you are allowed to stay in the UK indefinitely without restrictions, or the UK government has recognised you as a refugee (but not while you are an asylum seeker) or granted you humanitarian protection or discretionary leave to enter or remain in the UK. You do not meet them if your entry clearance to the UK says you have 'no recourse to public funds'. This is usually stamped in your passport or on your biometric residence permit. Universal credit counts as 'public funds'.

If you are unsure about how claiming might affect your position, get specialist immigration advice.

You must also be 'habitually resident' in the UK. This includes showing that you are settled in the UK and, usually, that you have been in the UK for at least one to three months. This also applies to British citizens returning to the UK from living abroad. Nationals of European Economic Area countries must have a 'right to reside' in the UK. Usually this means you are working or self-employed in the UK. These rules may change after the end of the transition period (due to end on 31 December 2020) following the UK's exit from the European Union.

EXAMPLE

Person from abroad

Mika fled her home country due to fear of persecution and has been recognised by the UK government as a refugee. She meets the immigration conditions because she has been granted refugee status and this also means she does not need to show that she is habitually resident in the UK. She is present in the UK and entitled to universal credit.

Are there other benefits for people from abroad?

There are special rules for certain groups of people from abroad for most other benefits.

Further information

There is more information about the rules for current benefits and tax credits in CPAG's *Welfare Benefits and Tax Credits Handbook*.

Appendix

Glossary of terms

Administrative penalty
A type of fine that can be offered to someone instead of being prosecuted, if the Department for Work and Pensions thinks a benefit offence may have been committed.

Alternative payment arrangements
The discretion to pay universal credit twice a month, directly to a landlord or split between partners.

Appointee
Someone, usually a relative, who is authorised by the Department for Work and Pensions to claim benefit on another person's behalf if that person cannot claim for her/himself – eg, perhaps because of a learning disability.

Assessment period
The monthly period on which universal credit payment is based. You are usually paid seven days after the end of each assessment period.

Bedroom tax
A reduction in the amount of the housing costs element for tenants of local authorities and housing associations who have a spare bedroom(s).

Benefit cap
The maximum amount of social security benefits that someone can receive. This includes most benefits, but there are some exceptions and some groups of people to whom the cap does not apply.

Budgeting advance
An advance payment of universal credit in the form of a loan, usually for people who have been on benefits for at least six months.

Capital
This includes savings, investments, certain lump-sum payments and property that is not a person's main home.

Care component
Part of disability living allowance paid if someone needs help looking after her/himself because of a disability or health problem.

Carer element
An extra amount of universal credit for people who care for a disabled adult or child.

Child element
An amount included in universal credit for someone responsible for child/ren.

Childcare costs element
An extra amount in universal credit for people in work who pay for childcare.

Civil penalty
A fine that can be imposed if someone is overpaid a benefit because s/he failed to provide information or gave incorrect information, and is not being prosecuted for fraud or another benefit offence.

Claimant commitment
A document setting out what someone must do while claiming universal credit, and the possible penalties if its terms are not met.

Conditionality
What claimants are required to do in return for their benefit.

Contributory benefit
A benefit for which entitlement depends on having paid a certain amount of national insurance contributions.

Couple
Two people living together who are married or civil partners, or living together as if they were a married couple.

Daily living component
Part of personal independence payment paid if someone has problems with daily living activities.

Disabled child addition
An extra amount of universal credit for a child or young person who gets disability living allowance or personal independence payment or who is blind.

Discretionary housing payment
A payment that can be made by a local authority to top up universal credit when someone needs extra help with her/his housing costs.

Earnings threshold
The amount of a person's earnings (or joint earnings for couples) above which there is no expectation to look for more work, or meet any other work-related requirements.

Elements
Amounts for children, disabilities, caring responsibilities, housing and childcare costs which make up part of a person's maximum universal credit award.

European Economic Area
The European Union member states, plus Iceland, Norway and Liechtenstein. For benefit purposes, Switzerland is also treated as part of the European Economic Area.

Flexible Support Fund
Department for Work and Pensions payments that can help people get, or stay in, work.

Friend and family carer
A person who has taken responsibility for a child of a friend or family member under a formal caring arrangement, or under an informal caring arrangement if it is likely s/he would otherwise be looked after by the local authority.

Habitually resident
Someone who has a settled intention to stay in the UK, and who has usually been living here for a period.

Hardship payments
Loans of universal credit made if someone's entitlement has been reduced by a sanction and s/he faces financial hardship.

Housing costs element
The amount of universal credit that helps with rent and certain service charges.

Independent Case Examiner
A body handling complaints about the Department for Work and Pensions.

Judicial review
A way of challenging the decisions of government departments, local authorities and some tribunals against which there is no right of appeal.

Legacy benefits
The benefits that are being replaced by universal credit: income support, income-based jobseeker's allowance, income-related employment and support allowance, housing benefit, child tax credit and working tax credit.

Limited capability for work element
An extra amount of universal credit paid to some people who are ill or disabled and who are not expected to work.

Limited capability for work test
A test of whether a person's ability to work is limited by a health condition such that s/he is not expected to work.

Limited capability for work-related activity element
An extra amount of universal credit paid to people who are too ill to prepare for work or who have a severe disability.

Limited capability for work-related activity test
A test of whether a person's health problems are so severe as to limit her/his ability to prepare for work.

Main carer
The person in a couple who spends the most time looking after the children, jointly nominated by the couple. The law refers to the 'responsible carer'.

Managed migration
The term used by the Department for Work and Pensions for the official process of transferring claimants to universal credit, not yet in operation in summer 2020 but due to be introduced in the near future.

Mandatory reconsideration
The requirement to have a decision looked at again by the Department for Work and Pensions before an appeal can be made.

Maximum universal credit
The amount of universal credit that someone is eligible for, before income is taken into account.

Means-tested benefit
A benefit that is only paid if someone's income and capital are low enough.

Minimum income floor
The amount of income a self-employed person is assumed to have, calculated by multiplying the national minimum wage by the number of hours s/he is expected to look for work.

National living wage
A set minimum hourly rate that employers must pay to people aged 25 or over.

National minimum wage
A set minimum hourly rate that employers must pay to people under 25.

Natural migration
The term used to describe the situation in which someone transfers to universal credit having decided to make a claim for it outside of the official managed migration process, usually following a change of circumstances for which s/he is unable to get the old means-tested benefits.

New-style employment and support allowance
A contributory form of employment and support allowance for those claiming under the universal credit system.

New-style jobseeker's allowance
A contributory form of jobseeker's allowance for those claiming under the universal credit system.

No recourse to public funds
A restriction that applies to some people subject to immigration control as part of their entry conditions to the UK, prohibiting them from claiming most benefits and tax credits, including universal credit.

Non-contributory benefit
A benefit for which entitlement does not depend on having paid a certain amount of national insurance contributions.

Non-dependant
An adult, other than a partner, who lives with the person claiming benefit – eg, a grown-up daughter or son.

Non-means-tested benefit
A benefit that is paid regardless of the amount of someone's income or capital.

Overpayment
An amount of benefit that is paid which is more than a person's entitlement.

Passporting
A term used to describe when entitlement to a particular benefit allows access to other benefits or sources of help.

Pension age
This is age 65, and will reach 66 by October 2020.

Person subject to immigration control
Someone who requires leave to enter or remain in the UK but does not have it, or who has leave to remain but is prohibited from having recourse to public funds, or has leave to remain in the UK on the basis of a sponsorship agreement.

Qualifying young person
A dependent young person aged 16 to 19 in full-time non-advanced education.

Real-time information
A system where employers send HM Revenue and Customs information about employees' earnings every time they are paid, which is then used by the Department for Work and Pensions to adjust universal credit awards.

Revision
A statutory method that allows benefit decisions to be changed.

Right to reside
A social security test, mainly affecting European Economic Area nationals, which must be satisfied in order to claim certain benefits.

Sanction
A reduction in a person's universal credit award for failing to meet her/his work-related requirements without a good reason or because s/he has committed an offence.

Sanction period
The length of time a sanction lasts for.

Severe disability premium
An extra amount in old means-tested benefits for someone who gets certain disability benefits, lives alone (or counts as living alone), and for whom no one gets carer's allowance.

Specified accommodation
Accommodation from a relevant body also providing care, support or supervision, or temporary accommodation provided because of domestic violence.

Standard allowance
The basic amount of universal credit paid for a single adult or a couple.

Supersession
A statutory method which allows benefit decisions to be changed, usually as a result of a change in circumstances.

Taper
The rate at which a person's maximum universal credit reduces as her/his earnings increase.

Temporary accommodation
Certain types of homeless accommodation where payments are made to a local authority or a social housing provider.

Transitional element
An additional amount of universal credit for people who are moved to universal credit under the managed migration process and whose universal credit award would be less than their previous benefits.

Transitional protection
A way of making sure that a person being transferred to universal credit under the official managed migration process from another benefit will not receive less money on universal credit than s/he did before.

Transitional SDP amount
A payment to compensate people who had a severe disability premium in their old benefit and have transferred to universal credit by 'natural migration' and have lost income as a result.

Two-child limit
A restriction on the number of child elements included in universal credit. There are exceptions – eg, if a child is adopted or for multiple births.

Universal credit advance
An advance of universal credit which can be paid if someone is in hardship while waiting for her/his first payment, if there is a delay in deciding someone's claim and in some other situations.

Universal support
Help to make or manage your claim and/or to budget.

Waiting period
The time before payment of certain elements can start.

Work allowance
The amount of earnings ignored before a person's universal credit award starts to be reduced. The amount depends on personal circumstances.

Work availability
One of the work-related requirements, which means being willing and able to take up paid work, usually immediately and within 90 minutes' travel time of home.

Work capability assessment
An assessment of whether someone has limited capability for work/ work-related activity.

Work coach
Someone employed by the Department for Work and Pensions to draw up claimant commitments, update them and check that claimants are meeting their work-related requirements.

Work-focused interview
One of the work-related requirements, which means attending an interview to discuss future work opportunities and the barriers to work.

Work preparation
One of the work-related requirements, which includes carrying out activities to prepare for a future return to work, such as increasing skills or doing a work placement.

Work-related requirements
The activities that a person must undertake to continue to receive the full amount of universal credit.

Work search
One of the work-related requirements, which means normally spending 35 hours a week looking for work.

Index

croyctax@croydon.gov.uk